ENDORSEMENTS

Resurrected Worth is a courageous story of redemption—one woman's journey from hidden pain to healing, from scarred endurance to restored wholeness. Constance André opens her heart with honesty and vulnerability, sharing the wounds, betrayals, and choices that shaped her life, and the profound hope she discovered in Jesus Christ, Who heals what feels beyond repair. As you walk beside her in her story, you are invited to reflect on your own journey and allow Christ to breathe new life into the places that once felt broken, revealing a beauty and worth found only in Him.

—DEBBIE VANCALSTEREN, beta reader

Constance's story is one not to be missed. Through raw honesty, deep vulnerability, and unwavering faith, she shows how God meets us in our pain and transforms it into healing and freedom. Her courage to openly reveal her fears, struggles, and testimony creates a powerful space for readers to encounter God's grace in a deeply personal way. I am not typically an avid reader, yet I found this book impossible to put down. Constance writes with authenticity and purpose, drawing readers in while continually pointing them back to God's redemptive power. She has a unique ability to connect with her audience, gently encouraging them to confront their own trauma, surrender it to Christ, and begin their own healing process. This book is not only engaging but also deeply impactful—reminding us that no pain is wasted in God's hands and that true transformation is possible through faith, obedience, and trust in Him. Constance's testimony is a reminder that God restores beauty from brokenness and uses our stories to provide hope and freedom to others.

—CRYSTAL PENNER, beta reader

Constance's compelling truth teaches readers the power of surrendering. A story of pain turned into salvation. This book will impact your soul with unwavering love. Challenges our faith to seek our worth in Christ. Despair transformed into freedom. The author reminds us of the choice we must make to follow God's purpose. Truly a gift from God. His masterpiece is in this beautiful testimony of resilience. Faith restored by truth, love, and most of all, God's healing hand.

—ELISHA ROSE, International Impact Book Award winner, two-time author, motivational speaker

Resurrected Worth

Before You Turn the Page ...
Set the Atmosphere.

This QR code contains the complete playlist curated to accompany *Resurrected Worth*—songs that shaped my healing journey and anchored me in truth.

Listen as you read.
Worship as you reflect.
Let every chapter be
wrapped in sound and Scripture.

Scan here for the full experience.

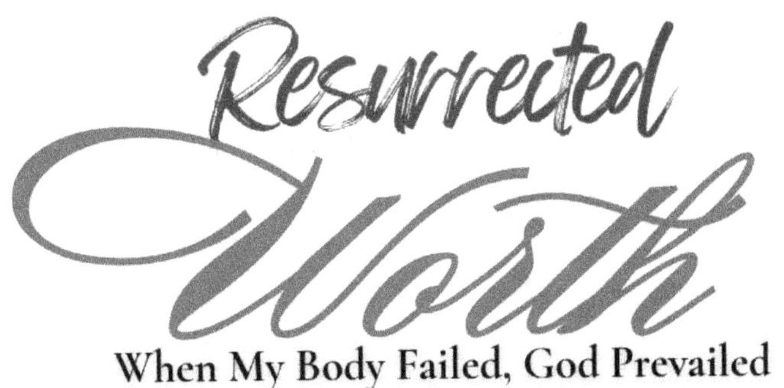

Resurrected Worth

When My Body Failed, God Prevailed

CONSTANCE ANDRÉ

Library of Congress Cataloging: 2026904802

Paperback: 978-1-956673-50-0

E-book: 978-1-956673-23-4

Hardback: 978-1-956673-24-1

Published by A Worthy Press, Chandler, Texas 75758, AWorthyPress.com

To protect the privacy of those who have shared their stories with the author, some details and names have been changed. Any "internet" addresses (websites, blogs, etc.) printed in this book are offered as a resource. They are not intended in any way to be or imply an endorsement by A Worthy Press, nor does A Worthy Press vouch for the content of these sites for the life of this book. This publication is designed to provide accurate and authoritative information in regard to the subject matter covered. The advice and strategies contained herein may not be suitable for your situation. You should consult with a professional when appropriate. Neither the publisher nor the author shall be liable for any loss of profit or any other commercial damages, including but not limited to special, incidental, consequential, personal, or other damages.

Scriptures marked (NIV) are taken from the Holy Bible, New International Version®, NIV®. Copyright © 1973, 1978, 1984, 2011 by Biblica, Inc.™ Used by permission of Zondervan. All rights reserved worldwide. www.zondervan.com The "NIV" and "New International Version" are trademarks registered in the United States Patent and Trademark Office by Biblica, Inc.™

Scripture quotations marked (NLT) are taken from the Holy Bible, New Living Translation, copyright ©1996, 2004, 2015 by Tyndale House Foundation. Used by permission of Tyndale House Publishers, Carol Stream, Illinois 60188. All rights reserved.

This book contains personal experiences and discussions related to trauma, emotional distress, and mental health. If you or someone you love is struggling with thoughts of self-harm or suicide, please seek immediate help.

In Canada or the United States, you can call or text 988, the Suicide & Crisis Lifeline, available 24 hours a day. If you are outside the United States, please contact your local emergency number or a trusted mental health professional. You are not alone, and help is available.

9-8-8: Suicide Crisis Helpline

Languages: English and French

CONTENTS

Foreword   1

Author's Note   5

Part One: Release   9

1. Anger   11

2. Obedience   29

3. Forgiveness   47

4. Control   65

Part Two: Reset   87

5. Abandonment   89

6. Rest   101

Part Three: Restore   109

7. Worth   111

8. Boundaries   137

9. Fear   147

10. Triggers   169

11. Emotions   189

Part Four: Rise   211

12. Patience   213

Epilogue   227

Acknowledgements   235

Music That Anchored My Healing   239

About the Author   245

Endnotes   248

DEDICATION

I dedicate this book to my Guiding Light and true Healer, God.

She was unstoppable, not because she did not have failures or doubts,
but because she continued on despite them.

—Beau Taplin

Foreword

Long before Jacob knew he was wrestling with God, he knew this—he could not let go. Many people wrestle, not realizing who they are wrestling with. You may be wrestling now, and that may be why you picked up this book. Or you may find yourself, as I did, beginning to wrestle as Constance shares her compelling story. The key is you haven't let go. You may feel like you want to, but as you read, you'll see again and again how God can use our pain for His glory. Wrestling can be holy work. God wastes nothing. Often, pain is the place of encounter.

From Genesis 32:22–32 (NLT), we know that Jacob had sent his family across the river. Alone in the darkness, he began wrestling with an unnamed opponent. His struggle lasted until daybreak, and while he left wounded, he was transformed by the encounter. We learn at the end of the story that Jacob wrestled with God.

This book is not about polished faith but about honest collision. (Pun intended. You'll have to keep reading the book.) You will witness transformation through surrender, and just as in Jacob's story, you'll see that the blessings come after Constance refuses to let go.

Through Jacob's example, the Bible (and thus God) permits us to wrestle with Him. Wrestling isn't a rebellion; it is engagement. It is growth.

As Constance digs out the roots that have entangled her heart, I pray you are brave enough to identify your roots. Is it anger, trauma, fear, silence, exhaustion, bitterness, jealousy, regret, or something so deep you haven't been able to pinpoint it?

Walking with Constance through the twelve roots that held her back from life and fully loving it, herself, and those around her, you will recognize areas in your life where you haven't fully healed. The practical exercises she uses will be tools you can utilize to position pain as the place where God meets us, not avoids us. Like Constance, you'll learn to lower your defenses and welcome trust.

This isn't a light read, but it is a page-turner. Your fellow wrestler, Constance, shares vulnerable moments from childhood to the present—moments most Christians wouldn't want to make known publicly. She rips off the mask of hypocrisy many Christians wear and confronts her past and present to show you the way out—the way to freedom physically, emotionally, and spiritually. In doing so, the woman who seemed strong to those around her turns her weaknesses into her greatest strengths.

The transformation that unfolds is not gentle. Jacob limps away; you may too. It's not just in Constance's telling of the stories but in the healing pathways that you may be reminded of roots you don't care to dig out. As you will see throughout this book, healing can hurt, expose, and disrupt everything you thought you knew or once held dear. When I began reading, she transported me to instances in my life that paralleled the trauma; she allowed me to do a gut check and clear the remaining debris.

As you begin, I invite you to take your time. If you feel the wrestling arise in your spirit, don't let go. Keep reading. Keep allowing God in the tension. This book is a safe place to lay down the burdens you were never meant to carry beyond the cross. Give yourself the space to confront and untangle the roots that surface as you actively engage in the healing process. While Constance wants you to observe her story to honor God and help you heal, it's not through resolution but through revelation—not through escape but an encounter. Remember, the joy and blessing come in the morning, but only if you don't let go.

—BRENDA A. HAIRE, author, speaker, and founder of Publish & Tell

AUTHOR'S NOTE

A Journey of Healing Deep-Rooted Pain

This book is based on four years of my life that led me to question everything I ever knew about myself and take a deep dive into healing the unknown.

Before the deep work God began, if you had asked me how complete healing is possible, I would have told you I never saw this coming. My healing journey may make you question several things you believe about yourself, others, emotions, the human body, and your faith in God.

Much of my journey has been discovering the roots that have shaped my life. God shed His light on *specific* roots through my journey: *Anger, Obedience, Forgiveness, Control, Abandonment, Rest, Worth, Boundaries, Fear, Triggers, Emotions,* and *Patience.*

In the middle of ordinary moments, God would quietly interrupt my thoughts with a single word. It arrived unannounced, yet it carried a weight I could not ignore. I knew He was inviting me to deal with something deeper. I may not have been able to explain what hearing God's voice feels like, but when He spoke, there was no confusion—I simply knew it was Him. Most often, I would hear Him while reading a self-help book of some kind, listening to inspirational music, or in the midst of an internal struggle while searching for clarity. After hearing the word, I would think about it, usually puzzled that it pertained to me. I would then proceed to have a conversation in my head, questioning if I felt the word held any merit, which often led to an internal argument. At first, I would deny I had an issue with the word, but while mulling it over and reflecting on it, more often than not, I would come to the realization that maybe there was something there to investigate. At times, a specific memory would rise to the surface, evidently connected to the root I was being called to process. I received it as a sign and moved forward in obedience.

As I accepted His challenge to begin digging up these roots, a revelation left me speechless: I had to dive into several aspects of my life to truly heal all physical pain tied to the roots God revealed. I uncovered triggers tied to past traumas, some from as early as four years old, which I had to process to heal and move forward as the child of God I am. In doing so, it helped alleviate my physical and emotional pain and allowed me to see my true worth for the first time in my life.

Throughout my journey, God spoke to me through songs. At just the right moments, they were songs whose messages I needed to hear to lift my spirit, for a revelation or an aha moment, for encouragement and deep healing, or simply to give me hope. Songs that pierced as if God were whispering the lyrics to me, or which I found myself saying to release how I felt. Music consistently nourishes my soul and is one of my go-tos, no matter my emotional state. This is why I have chosen to include some meaningful songs along with the account of my healing journey.

I hope to convey to you how I physically healed with God's guidance by uncovering and addressing the root issues in my life. To do so, I had to understand how I became the person I grew up to be. I had to learn how to uncover the buried aspects of my inner self, to be open to ripping off the bandages, and to face *all* trauma, as well as to be open to change, which often meant a journey over a rough and pain-filled road. I had to embrace pain and suffering in order to heal. When I think of roots, I think of the nourishment one needs to grow and thrive. If there are roots that are holding you hostage within yourself, as mine were, let me clearly say to you, "It's time to break free!"

Buckle up! I'm sure there will be tears of sadness and joy mixed with some laughter as you read through the journey of how I faced the battle within me with courage, an open mind, understanding, and resilience. Liberally sprinkled, I admit, with outrage, uncertainty, and resistance. Even though at times I could not see hope or purpose, I embarked on the once unimaginable to become the best version of myself. My true, authentic self.

If you allow it to, this journey will move you to your core. I pray the Holy Spirit will empower and inspire you—speaking to your soul because of my journey—and that God will use my pain as His platform to spark something beautiful in you. As we walk together, allow God to use my healing to heal and inspire you to find your authentic self. Feel free to stain the pages with tears. Mark, highlight, and write in the margins. Don't be afraid to bring the roots we discuss to the surface; that is where the soil is the richest! I will be with you each step of the way.

A cautionary note: please do not compare your trauma with mine or anyone else's. Each person experiences trauma in their own way and at different levels. All trauma, regardless of its form, deserves healing just the same.

Part One: Release

I needed to release the pain, the blame, and the need to understand why so I could truly heal.

—Constance André

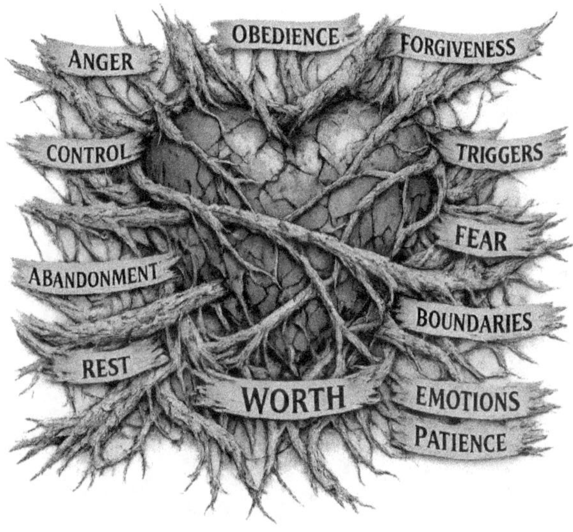

Chapter One

ANGER

The most difficult thing is the decision to act.
The rest is merely tenacity.

—Amelia Earhart

Anger is a complex word when you truly think about it, even though the actions that often go along with it can be rather quick and careless.

You have heard the saying, "Sticks and stones may break my bones, but names will never hurt me." Well, I'm here to tell you that the words that come out of someone's mouth in anger or rage *can* destroy the person to whom they are directed. I experienced this firsthand. I have witnessed anger my entire life, along with the destructive patterns that it has caused to myself and to others. I wish I could say I stood only on the receiving end of it, but unfortunately, that is not the case. I've seen people's spirits crushed, relationships destroyed, suicide attempts, and personally, I've felt the desperate fear and the trembling that it caused in my own life.

Anger is a generational sin in my family, something I thought I would struggle with my entire life. I thought I was just born this way; this is how it is; I have to discover a way to deal and cope with it. I did not realize there are tools nowadays, other than anger management, to help us understand what is indeed going on. Don't get me wrong. I have sought help in this area numerous times in my life, but I constantly seem to struggle with anger. I can't tell you the number of times I've prayed for God to remove my anger. For decades, I would ask that of Him only to discover myself angry when the next expectation or need was unmet.

I don't know about you, but I will be the first to acknowledge that anger was my go-to for far too long. It did not matter the situation: relationships, family, my daughter, or work. When I became overwhelmed and my expectations were not met, anger arose instantly to protect me like a jacket from the cold. Anger often rises as a distorted form of self-protection—an emotional shield we raise against real or perceived hurt, masking the pain or fear stirring beneath.

In the past, when I thought of seeking help and seeing a counsellor, I would criticise myself, fear someone seeing me as weak or tell myself that I did not really need help. The phrases that often ran through my mind (or should I say *excuses,* if I'm honest) were "it's not for me," "I don't need to change," "so and so is the issue, not me," "I have every right to be angry," and so on.

Well, let me be very clear that while I'm a very capable, independent, strong-minded individual, I had to be willing to surrender. I had to be vulnerable and seek help so that I could break the generational cycle for my husband and daughter to live without anger tormenting them and to have a healthy wife and mother. Ending the cycle started with me, no matter the cost. It turns out my willingness to be vulnerable released me from physical and emotional pain, allowing me to become the person God intended me to be. I began to see that it takes courage to step up and step out, to ask for help, because that's not the go-to for me. By picking up this book, you, too, must be at the place where courage meets vulnerability. Hang with me. What God revealed to me transformed me, and now He is allowing me the opportunity to bless you with the same tools. Which of the phrases above sounds uncomfortably familiar to you? Have you ever chosen to struggle in silence—convinced that asking for help would make you look weak?

Too many times, I would try with everything in me to rectify a situation, a health crisis, you name it, before I would seek God in prayer and ask for help. You would think I would have learned my lesson over the years, but surrendering control doesn't come easily to me to this day.

In the fall of 2022, I worked up the courage to seek help. My professional counsellor asked me to read the book *Overcoming Emotions that Destroy: Practical Help for Those Angry Feelings That Ruin Relationships.*[1] Well, doesn't the title just say it all? As I read, I thought the title was true in every aspect. Let me tell you, this book slapped me upside the face, woke me up, and essentially told me I had to dig out what was feeding my root of anger. I cried more than I care to admit while reading the book, but this was where my journey had to start. I have read the book three times, and every time, new phrases stir something different within me. Each reread reveals another layer of growth—proof that God has grown wisdom in me. I bravely stepped into what He asked of me, even when it was uncomfortable, meant change, and was painfully hard to do. God used this book to change my life! I strongly encourage you to read it if you're struggling with your emotions or anger. Is anger at the root of the pain in your life? You can't heal from what you don't acknowledge.

Even though I sought help, I could not understand what was genuinely going on or what was causing my anger to grow. Call me naive, but I did not know emotions lie beneath the surface and that anger is similar to the iceberg principle, a mere symptom of something deeper. Trauma is an iceberg. The part the world sees—the anger, the fear, the shut-down moments—is only the visible fracture. Underneath the surface lie the hidden wounds, the beliefs, and the buried stories that shape everything above the waterline. Often, what lies beneath is more cumbersome than what others can see or we can fathom.

> It is vitally important to understand anger is the outside emotion sent to protect the inner, more sensitive aspects of our hearts. It's a secondary response that hides a deeper or more sensitive issue. When people abandon us, when they let us down, when someone doesn't come through, when we feel rejected, left out, lonely, sad, or sorrowful, we generally cover it up with anger. Because these emotions are so strong, painful, and confusing, anger serves as a more satisfying substitute.[2]

As I read those words, situations and emotions began to make sense. The concepts resonated deeply as I visualized a heart hidden below the surface, buried in the shadows where no one looks. Roots—old wounds, lies, and unhealed pain—wrap around it like chains choking the life God intended for it to carry. It's almost as if the words jumped off the page and were now embedded in my brain so that I could understand and process all the situations and trauma I had faced.

While reading, I came across questions that did not sit well with me and got my undivided attention. Here is a quotation from Chapter 1, "Hope for our Anger":

Have you Ever...?
Have you ever done something you wished you hadn't when you were angry?
Have you ever said something when you were angry you wish you could take back?
Have you ever made a bad decision when you were angry?
Have you ever ruined a friendship, a marriage, a family relationship, a ministry relationship, or a business relationship because of anger?
Have you ever seen a person hurt because of someone's anger physically, emotionally or psychologically?[3]

As I reflected on the questions and the fact that I could say yes to all of them, I knew I had an anger problem. How are you feeling after reading the questions? Any of them prick your heart? The last question hit me where it hurt the most. My anger has wounded people I care about physically, emotionally, and/or psychologically. It is painful when I reflect on how deeply anger shaped the way I handled situations. But I am done hiding behind excuses. I am owning my mistakes fully, and I am actively seeking the help I have desperately needed. My actions were shameful. If you are feeling shame because of your anger, know that God doesn't shame us. He meets us with correction, clarity, and an invitation to heal. You don't usually step onto a healing path with confidence. Sometimes you step forward simply because staying where you are hurts more. That is where I was—moving ahead without answers, knowing my heart needed serious reconstruction.

Overcoming Emotions states that "anger isn't bad or wrong. It's a signal that something is uncomfortable, wrong, or undesirable."[4] That is exactly how I would describe the feeling when I would get angry. "Uncomfortable" is where the source of my anger started, but why? Anger meant I felt emotions that I did not care to feel. I remained still, confused as a new revelation came to light.

Anger can initially rise to defend what matters, although it often becomes an unhealthy way to protect ourselves. Too often, it becomes a shield we hide behind—one that keeps us from facing our deeper wounds. Instead of facing the real issue, we use anger to avoid vulnerability. When we don't want to expose the deeper issues of our hearts or wrestle with the inner work God desires to do, anger becomes our refuge. By fixating on anger, we avoid confronting the true source of our pain. Many may cling to anger as a weapon, fearing that releasing anger means releasing accountability. The truth is, anger holds immense power—it can either deepen our bondage or lead us toward freedom.

As I pondered the truth behind every word I read, I was speechless, utterly speechless, as the phrases hit hard. I sensed more than ever that God wanted to heal me, and I had to uncover the roots of my anger. It's almost as if God were holding up a big billboard in front of my face, asking me to see the sign. He had opened the door, and I needed to walk through it, no matter what would be revealed or what it would cost me.

This unfortunately meant that I would be left raw and gutted as God exposed the hidden wounds that had been feeding my root of anger.

As I continued reading, the next few chapters of *Overcoming Emotions* explained the "faces of anger": spewer, stuffer, leaker. A *spewer* releases anger outwardly—through sharp words, harsh tones, or explosive actions. A *stuffer* pushes emotions down, pretending nothing is wrong while quietly carrying the weight inside. A *leaker*, however, allows anger to seep out slowly, disguising it through sarcasm, criticism, withdrawal, or procrastination, all while resentment and bitterness continue to take root beneath the surface. I recognized that I am mostly a spewer and leaker, but really, I wear all three faces. I thought, *How is it possible to have all three faces of anger within one person?* I soon understood that everyone has all three, and we must learn to balance and use them correctly for justified anger.

For someone who doesn't care to read much, I found myself reading more than ever to try to understand what went wrong and where. I would read the emotions book and reflect during the week, and at the next meeting with my counsellor, we would discuss how I reacted to what I had read.

I have underlined, starred, and highlighted so much of this book that the publisher wouldn't recognize it. Things that really spoke to me, resonated with me, or which I knew I had to directly deal with, I highlighted pink so that I could easily reference them. Going back in time to deal with my trauma was not a straightforward process. It took me time, soul searching, and God's guidance to be fully committed to opening the door to the deep, deep wounds I bear. However, I fully trusted God to walk with me through this painful journey, to give me strength, and to hold me up when I could not stand. *Overcoming Emotions* states, "You can be a sincere Christian and still have problems with spewing. Rather than considering yourself hopelessly aggressive, simply realize that you have never learned to deal with anger constructively and begin that process now."[5] These words resonate with me and give me hope. Situations were placed into perspective as to why I've struggled with anger. Right after I read the above quote, I made a decision. I was going to learn how to deal with my anger constructively and to rectify the wrongs I had done in my life. I knew my mission, as hard as it was going to be, would one day be rewarding when I did not have to carry all the baggage anymore. I can now tell you, it may not be easy, but it will be worth it.

As I sought direction, I often read my Bible, and a passage that made a huge impact on me is James 1:19–22 (NLT):

> *Understand this, my dear brothers and sisters: you must all be quick to listen, slow to speak, and slow to get angry. Human anger does not produce the righteousness God desires. So get rid of all the filth and evil in your lives, and humbly accept the word God has planted in your hearts, for it has the power to save your souls. But don't just listen to God's word. You must do what it says. Otherwise, you are only fooling yourselves.*

That's a pretty direct passage to try and live up to. I don't know about you, but I felt as if I would fail daily. However, I decided to try to be quick to listen, slow to speak, and slow to become angry just as God asked. For some people, this might be very simple; however, for me, this was extremely hard and something I had to apply conscious effort to.

As issues started coming to light in my counselling sessions, we discussed them using narrative therapy. Narrative therapy, which involves writing letters, seemed to work very well for me. I wrote several letters to people who had caused deep-seated pain that I carried in my mind and body. I wrote letters to family members: my father, mother, husband, multiple friends throughout my life, my inner child, and more. Yes, that's right, my inner child. I wrote several letters to a younger version of myself.

I recall sitting in my bedroom multiple nights over the next few months with a box of tissues beside me, emotions streaming down my cheeks, pouring my heart and soul into the ink that I scratched onto the paper, hardly able to see through the tears. Each letter held every emotion embedded deep within and attached to the trauma that had taken place. I released it all. All my thoughts, fears, and heartache came out into the open. I did not hold anything back. At this point, I thought, *What do I have to lose?* I would often ask questions in the letters as I wanted answers as well. Some of these letters cut so deep they pulled me back into the trauma, forcing me to relive it all over again. When I opened a painful situation in my heart and mind to be able to release all the emotion tied to it, I was left feeling exposed.

Unfortunately, my 10-year-old daughter witnessed several evenings of me crying uncontrollably as if my heart were being ripped out of my body. One thing I know for sure is that I needed to process my anger through narrative therapy so I could truly release the emotional pain that was attached. I was pleasantly surprised by how refreshed I felt the day after pouring it all out on the page, even though my eyes were so swollen I looked as if I'd had an allergic reaction. I experienced a sense of peace, and I knew that I had dealt with the trauma. It was laid to rest. I must say it was the weirdest feeling, and truth be told, I don't even know how to fully comprehend it—to discern the peace but to be so wounded and fragile at the same time.

As a mother, I could not really tend to my daughter's needs as I could hardly tend to my own during these times. I felt completely broken. I'm sure what she witnessed during these times has impacted her in ways that I cannot even fathom. She would sometimes sneak into my room and snuggle with me, reassuring me that everything would be okay as we prayed together. I am certain she said numerous prayers of her own for what she experienced because life as we knew it had turned upside down.

When I managed to pull myself together, I was able to explain to her what I was doing and why I was doing it. I sat her down. Looking into her beautiful blue eyes, with tears streaming down my face, I explained to the best of my ability what I felt and why I had ventured down this road. You may not choose to share this openly with your children; however, my loving daughter is very mature for her age, and I wanted to raise her in truth and love. I knew I was fractured and that in my stripped-down state, I often hurt those I love, including her. I did not want to cause harm to anyone any longer and was finally getting help, and this is what help looked like. My hope and prayer is that she will follow in the same steps of healing if she needs to.

As time went by, I started to heal, and my outlook began to shift. I noticed that I responded differently to situations. I've changed how I guide my daughter in life, how I encourage her to deal with uncomfortable situations as they come up, and how I encourage her to seek help immediately. I understand that my child is a sponge, and what she witnesses in life, and especially behind closed doors, will shape her character for the future. My life has been shaped by trials—abuse and traumas—I did not choose, and I pray she will not have to walk the same fragmented path that once defined me. I want to protect her and give her the best life possible, which starts with me healing at my core.

My counsellor once connected the letters I wrote to release traumatic events with an illustration I will never forget. He stated, "Think of it like a waitress. You sit down, she takes your order, and when you're done with your food, she brings you the bill. You pay the bill, and as soon as you have paid, it's out of her head, and she doesn't look back but rather moves on to the next table." These wise words resonated deeply because they were undeniably true. I had to release the anger, pain, and emotion consuming my mind so I would stop dwelling on the frightening actions I'd endured and free myself to move forward with healing. These letters were the release my heart longed for so that the anger would no longer dwell in my mind. I did not share them with anyone and even burnt some of them as they were not intended for anyone to see. I wrote them to open the door to the healing that needed to take place.

Let me be clear; the anger-fueled moments I'm about to describe are not my finest moments, but I believe I need to be completely vulnerable so you can comprehend the power of true transformation. Truth be told, I'm rather ashamed that I struggled with anger as long as I did, considering I previously worked hard to overcome it. I will, however, give myself a pat on the back and the same grace God gives. I'm pleased with the strides I've made.

I strongly agree that "anger is a secondary emotion that hides deeper issues. It's the light on the dashboard that signals that something is wrong under the hood. It's the way we protect ourselves from hurt, frustration, and insecurity."[6] That revelation hit home as I began learning the skills to manage my anger.

I began to see that when my anger surfaced, I had to pause and identify its source. I would ask myself, "What about my situation caused this emotion to rise?" Part of this discovery process meant talking to myself. It felt weird at first—maybe even a little uncomfortable; I won't deny that. But in those moments of honest reflection, I started to see how present situations were stirring old, unresolved emotions that were quietly being fueled. The following is one scenario I had to work through, and I've included the steps I used to process my response—my anger.

First, I would recognize that I was angry. Then I'd ask the question, "Why am I angry?"

Answer: I asked Dave to spend time with us, and here Raelyn and I are all alone.

I would then ask, "What emotion am I feeling?"

Answer: I'm feeling unheard, unloved, rejected, invisible, like a piece of furniture.

Then I would take one of those words and process it further. "Why am I not feeling heard?"

Answer: Dave did not show up.

I asked myself, "Why does that make me angry?"

Answer: I have constantly been left behind. My voice has

not mattered. No one has heard what I had to say. I was left out, pushed aside, not chosen.

And finally, the source surfaced: a cycle of neglect that led me to a specific situation that kept stirring this emotion. Sometimes, if I close my eyes while I process my anger, I can see an image of exactly what is tied to the emotion. I keep talking until I know I am at the source. To succeed in this task, I have to be open-minded and willing to go places that hurt. When we want to stop, we need to keep pushing to identify the root. After implementing this powerful tool in several different situations, the revelations shook me. I discovered anger was linked to an emotion that I had held in my body from a childhood trauma I had not yet dealt with.

For years leading up to this healing, I sought help through professionals and prayer so that I would no longer be that angry person, but as I've always said to others, "What's in the heart comes out of the mouth." Jesus confirms this in Matthew 12:34b (NIV), "For the mouth speaks what the heart is full of." Yet it did not occur to me to reflect on my own heart and my own issues.

Even though my heart holds joy and happiness in many areas, I, like most people, carry scars and have those closets where I hide things—both from others and from myself. For me, those scars stemmed from trauma that stirred deep emotions and anger within.

As I continued counselling, I was repeatedly struck by new insights. I learned that I often build brick walls instead of fences, seeing the world as black and white with no shades of gray. These words were familiar to me. Over the years, I've had several close friends direct them to me, but it took the validation from the certified professional to stop dismissing them.

I recall my counsellor asking me why there can't be gray areas. When I examined the origin of this belief, my longing for security revealed itself. Believing decisions are black and white equated to security, and gray areas led to feelings of uncertainty, which meant I felt unsafe. I did not want to feel the emotions that were tied to these painful areas in my life. They were gut-wrenching, so in essence, I erected a brick wall and ran the other way so I could escape and protect myself. In hindsight, it is similar to "the stuffer" mentioned in the book *Overcoming Emotions*. However, this behavior that I had developed to protect myself destroyed several relationships and is not a healthy way to deal with trauma!

I eventually recognized that the brick walls I built served as a survival mechanism—formed as early as four years old, when trauma met emotions I had no capacity to process. That is the age when my brain switched to survival mode, and nothing else mattered. Talking about what happened was not accepted in my family, and things were just buried underneath the proverbial rug; life kept going as if the damage didn't exist. This survival mechanism became normal for me, and I hid my pain in my self-made brick fortress my entire life. I froze in time at four years of age. I survived; however, it created a massive pit that I had to climb out of.

As my counsellor and I peeled back the layers of trauma, I understood that when my great-grandfather returned after World War II, there would have been post-traumatic stress disorder (PTSD) that no one recognized. Unfortunately, my grandfather endured PTSD-induced violence, which he then took out on my father, and my father acted on all that he experienced so that I, in turn, endured violence as I grew up.

As I put the pieces together, I began to recognize that my father did the best he could with what he knew and that he himself needed the help that I'd finally sought. I know in my heart that my father felt several of the same emotions I felt, but he simply did not know how to deal with them, as he, too, was not equipped.

Through my healing journey, I also learned that anger is directly linked to our needs and expectations. It is crucial to understand that when we feel hurt, quite often that is a reflection of our needs not being met. When we are hurting, anger naturally rises within. The second source of anger is unmet expectations: "When things don't go the way we want . . . we get frustrated. When plans change unexpectedly, when goals are blocked, when dreams are dashed, and hopes are abandoned, anger is fast on the heels. Our expectations set us up for disappointment when they are unrealistic."[7] Reading this section in *Overcoming Emotions* created a lightbulb moment for me. For the first time in my life, I saw how everything connected.

I recognized that if I was going to grow, I needed to ask myself if I had any unmet expectations or needs in my life. Did I have any unresolved issues that I had to face and work through? Anger didn't have to control me. Instead of ruling me, my anger began to inform me. In God's hands, it became a tool—drawing my attention to the unseen roots in my heart that needed healing.

As I started freeing myself from anger, I had to pick out all the weeds that were tied to the roots that had grown deep in my life. Beneath layers of trauma and perhaps even some denial, I would often uncover a source, a root. Sometimes, I had to revisit the same situation multiple times to release all the anger and emotion associated with a trauma. Facing the very wounds I tried to outrun could feel terrifying, but that is where I had to start my journey—breaking down my brick wall. Speaking from experience, if you don't seek the source of your anger, you *will* be a prisoner to your anger for life. You will dig yourself a deeper hole than you ever thought imaginable. Unfortunately, this is where I had to start, at the rock bottom of a deep pit.

Life's circumstances play a critical role in anger. Quite often, I found myself stewing over what had been done to me—unfair moments that left me hurt, even deeply sad. Over time, I came to accept that life itself is not fair. Yet instead of processing the pain, laying it to rest, and moving forward, I would thought-stack, digging myself into a deeper pit of hurt and sometimes layering it with feelings of betrayal.

A wise person once told me that I have a choice: I can respond the way I normally would, or I can choose to take a different path and do something different.

I'm sure everyone has been treated unfairly or unjustly at some point in their lives. I'm sure we have all had hurt feelings, our pride affected negatively, our toes stepped on, and our thoughts dismissed. But at the end of the day, we have a choice, and we can choose anger or choose to handle the situation better than we ever would have.

As I leaned on God to continue healing my root of anger, I submerged myself in Scripture. Even though I felt defeated in this process more times than I can count, I kept looking up to God, pleading for His help and for Him to end all the pain and suffering I felt. I found comfort and clung to the words in Jeremiah 29:11 (NIV), "'For I know the plans I have for you,' declares the LORD, 'plans to prosper you and not to harm you, plans to give you hope and a future.'" The words "prosper you and not to harm you" became my lifeline.

My curiosity had been piqued, and I had to understand why I allowed things to bother me the way they did, identify the root source of every trauma I endured, and process it fully so I could release the pain and allow God's plans to unfold.

In essence, I had to change my mindset. I chose to quit playing the victim, to start looking in the mirror and take ownership of my actions. When I started dissecting the real issues at hand, I started truly healing.

Dissection is a painful process. It hurts. It's going to take some guts to get through, but with God as my guiding light, it's by far the most rewarding thing I've ever done in my life. The peace I feel because I dealt with my root of anger is like nothing I have ever experienced. And it's available to you too. Although it was a long, painful process, I would do it all over again if need be.

Words cannot truly express how much the book *Overcoming Emotions* impacted the course of my life. I simply cannot speak highly enough of the book. That book is not just for individuals who struggle with anger; it's for any person who walks the face of this earth. There is such valuable insight and knowledge in that book. I will be forever grateful to my counsellor for recommending *Overcoming Emotions* as part of my healing journey. If your brick wall is as high as mine was, I encourage you to take a deep dive. My "CliffsNotes" simply don't do it justice.

If you need support, I encourage you to reach out and allow me to help you through this process. Please do not venture down this road alone. More importantly, God will give you the courage to dig deep and face whatever anger and emotion lies beneath if you look to Him for guidance. When you allow God to lead, He will transform you from the inside; just wait and see.

I reflected deeply on all that I went through and read. Could some of my anger be linked to my unwillingness to accept who I was or was not? Did I have roots stemming from my own unwillingness? Perhaps what I needed most was not more answers but the courage to step out in obedience.

Please scan the QR code to explore the songs that spoke to my heart while healing my root of anger.

Chapter Two

OBEDIENCE

Obedience is an act of faith; disobedience is the result of unbelief.

—Edwin Louis Cole

January 2021 arrived without warning. One morning, I opened my eyes and knew—before my feet touched the floor—that something had gone terribly wrong. My body no longer obeyed me. The simple act of standing sent the room tilting. I reached for furniture, walls—anything solid—to keep from falling. My thoughts moved through fog. Dizziness lingered. Fatigue pressed down like a weight I could not shake. My blood pressure dropped, my pulse lowered, and the numbers only deepened my fear. Every signal pointed in the same direction, whispering a frightening possibility: my heart might be failing.

My health had deteriorated to the point that some days at work, when I tried to focus, the monitor would seem to shake. Other times, I would look at something, but my brain could not connect the dots as quickly as normal. Trying to shake it off, I shook my head, closed my eyes, and blinked several times as if I was seeing things, but this could not be shaken off. Several doctors, lots of blood work, and a few emergency room visits later, there was no explanation of my sudden decline. They tested me with halter monitors, ECGs, and echocardiograms, but nothing showed up that would cause these types of issues. Next came the cardiologist referral. As I anxiously awaited the appointment, my mind ran rampant with its own diagnoses.

During my first meeting with the cardiologist, he reviewed my file and recommended adding salt to my diet to raise my blood pressure, explaining it should alleviate my symptoms. Shocked, I questioned his advice because we've been told that too much salt is not good for us and could cause weight gain. After struggling with my weight my entire life, I didn't need to gain any. He answered, "A little weight gain shouldn't be your main concern if it fixes the problem." His response dumbfounded me. This could not be the solution to resolve the awfulness I felt. This sounded like a bunch of nonsense, and I refused to accept his solution. I left his office disappointed that I had waited this long for a specialist who recommended nothing of value.

My health continued to deteriorate, peaking with chest pains forcing me to leave work and drive to the emergency room. *What is going on with me?! What is happening?! This is not normal; this is not how I should be acting; I am only thirty-nine years old.* Upon arriving at the emergency room, another ECG, more blood tests, and a heart ultrasound yet *again* revealed nothing—no heart issues and no other abnormalities. The doctor told me that my heart was as fit as an athlete's and there were no concerns. Puzzled because I'm physically in no shape to be an athlete, I could not believe that those words came out of his mouth. Most people would be excited to hear that their heart is as fit as an athlete's, but for me, this meant we were still at ground zero with diagnosing the problem.

This phase of my health issues lasted about three and a half months. With life as I knew it robbed from me, I felt severely aged and hardly able to function. Looking back on these events, I understand now that I had an anxiety attack. I would have never admitted this to myself back then because, in my mind, it could not happen to me; I truly believed this. I think we've all been there at one time or another where we feel invincible or that circumstances don't physically affect us. After all, it "always happens to other people," doesn't it? It was a difficult lesson to accept that the problem was internal, tied to my mindset, and genuinely affecting me.

After realizing that anxiety can trigger symptoms that mimic life-threatening illness, I knew I needed to find the cause of my anxiety. Unsure if it was physical or mental, I took my friend's suggestions to try a B12 supplement. We discussed my symptoms and how I felt, and in my head, I ruled it out as a possibility because the doctors tested my blood for B12 and it came back in the normal range. You see, at this point, numerous people were giving me their advice and ideas, trying to help, but it got very irritating when nothing was working, yet everyone seemed to have the solution. I constantly felt torn and pulled in several different directions; I was at my wits' end and feeling like rubbish. A simple walk to the grocery store to grab a few things and head back to the car left me completely played out. However, I thought about it and decided I had nothing to lose and reluctantly ventured out to buy some B12.

To my amazement, on day four, it was as if a light switch was turned on, and I felt normal. *What on earth?* I thought, *How is this possible?!* After everything they had tested me for, how could a simple vitamin be fixing how I was feeling? Nonetheless, I was incredibly thankful for this friend and made sure I expressed my gratitude to her.

Some may say I am a strong-willed individual, and when my mind is set on something, well, let's just say it's not easily swayed. Unfortunately, this can be a blessing, and sometimes this can be a curse. My stubbornness kept me from listening to others' diagnoses of my symptoms, especially after the doctor ruled out a B12 deficiency. Too often, we allow our mindset or thoughts to stand in the way of positive outcomes. I am guilty of this, and unfortunately, I had to learn the hard way after three and a half months of suffering.

Even though B12 solved a slew of unbelievable health issues, it did not relieve stress in my life. I found myself stretched beyond my limits. I had my hands in three different companies while completing administrative and accounting duties. If it's asked of me, by nature, I would just get it done, no questions. I completed the work. What I didn't know was that this work ethic negatively affected my health at a rapid rate.

Although I asked for help, as I felt buried at times, it took a long while to secure help, and the workload kept depleting me further and further. On several evenings, I sank into my deck chair, poured a glass of wine, and tried to cope. Fatigue hollowed me out, numbness took over, and beneath the surface, everything inside me splintered. I knew I could not keep this up. I did not see how my emotions brewed internally. The feelings of anger, frustration, hurt, and rejection were beginning to overwhelm me. I would hold all these emotions in as I felt I could not show them on my face, something I learned from a very young age.

Although I thought I did a good job at covering things up, in hindsight, what transpired was the worst thing I could have ever done for my health.

That April, I experienced my first panic attack driving home from work. As opposed to the slow build-up and lingering anxiety attack I'd previously experienced, this occurred suddenly and left me feeling disabled. Earlier that day, I'd had a meeting with one of my superiors about some concerns with an individual I was training. What I had anticipated as a meeting to plan the training for this individual quickly turned into complaints that I was being disrespectful, uncooperative, and rude to management. As I listened to these words, I sat in disbelief, my heart laid bare and devastated. My whole life, I've strived to be an upright, honest, loyal, dependable person who treats others the way I want to be treated. Feeling crushed, I had an extremely hard time coping with what I heard. Devastated, I felt as if she could not be talking about me. I could not fathom hearing these complaints about myself. It didn't equate with my life's mantra and how I thought I presented myself. As I sat, confronted and defeated, I broke down sobbing and apologizing for anything I did that caused them to see me this way, as I did not even recognize the person she described. That is not the person I am or have ever been, and the fact that I could not see it, but others on the outside looking in could, meant that there was a bigger issue at hand.

About a mile from home, the panic attack hit. The entire drive home, I'd replayed every moment in my mind, desperate to understand what they accused me of and why. No matter how hard I tried, I could not make sense of it. I thought my supervisor's comments misrepresented the situation and didn't reflect my true character. I started hyperventilating, felt tightness in my chest, and could not catch my breath. I called my best friend but could not reach her, so I became frantic with no one to assist me. I felt as though I were drowning and had no lifeline. I managed to pull my car over and phoned my sister-in-law, but I could hardly release the words through the sobs to explain what was happening. I could sense she knew what I was experiencing, and she eventually talked me through it and calmed me down. You see, I was constantly the rock—steady, dependable, the one everyone leaned on. But under the mounting pressure and stress of my own life, I felt myself spiraling. The version of me I had unfailingly known was crumbling, and I no longer recognized who I was becoming. I felt completely lost. Questions echoed endlessly in my mind: *Who am I now? What is the purpose of my life?* The deeper I spiralled, the more hope slipped through my fingers, until hopelessness was the only thing that remained.

Shortly after the panic attack, a dear friend told me maybe it's time to look for a different career and switch jobs. I responded with "Yeah, right, as if that's ever going to happen," and shot the idea down as it came out of her mouth. I'd been at the company for nearly ten years by this time, so changing careers did not seem like a possibility to me. It meant *change*. Accepting change has not been my strong suit. Since my brain was stuck in survival mode from a young age, it became programmed for safety. This, unfortunately, meant being in the fight, flight, or freeze response at all times. Keeping everything the same—frozen—was part of survival for me.

As I continued to struggle with stress, more and more friends were stating the obvious, sharing their thoughts, and telling me to put myself first. I repeatedly heard, "No job is worth what this is doing to your health." When I look back, I see the signs were all there, and my friends could *clearly* see them, but as the saying goes, "From the inside looking out, you can never see how it looks from the outside looking in."

Unfortunately, the despair continued, and I felt as if my hard-working spirit died. What my superiors could remember were the negatives, which I still don't agree with to this day. Isn't that the truth for each of us, though? We are programmed to identify the mistakes and remember the negatives. In doing so, we conveniently forget the positives. I am guilty of this, which is why I'm an excellent accountant. I'm used to finding mistakes. I have to consciously work on finding the positives in all situations. Some days, this is a real challenge for me; however, I have learned to change my mindset and focus on what's essential. I usually ask myself if my thoughts are uplifting someone or tearing them down. By doing so, I can divert conflict. Which is why I had a really tough time coming to grips with how they represented me during that meeting. Miserable and drowning in work, I trained person after person while expected to keep up my regular duties, which was nearly impossible. Even with incredible stress, I did not want to fail; I did not want to show weakness; and I did not want to be seen as incompetent. So, I put my head down, working as quickly as possible, without mistakes, without breaks, to accomplish everything they asked of me.

In late August, as I read my morning devotional by Stormie Omartian in *The Power of a Praying Woman,* the words really struck me.[8] They appeared as if they were jumping off the page in bold lettering. Have you ever read something so profound that you knew the words were penetrating your soul? Well, those words penetrated my soul as if I were having a conversation with God Himself.

For about three weeks, everything I read left me questioning my life. It didn't matter what I read. My daily desk calendar, my devotional, and random sections in the Bible I flipped to all aligned and pointed in the same direction. I questioned what I was doing with my life, my health, and my family. I started some deep soul searching. Did I truly desire to listen and be obedient to what God wanted to teach me, or would I continue to play it safe and keep myself in this cycle of people pleasing? As I mulled over the choices, I fought an internal battle during a few turbulent weeks. My root of obedience came reluctantly—I knew God knew better, yet I still fought Him. What He asked of me reshaped my life entirely.

As I leaned into God and explored what He asked of me, I began to see that the love I once had for my job was no longer there, and it was, in fact, turning into bitterness. I found myself talking about work issues with my friends and seeking advice, something I did not initiate previously. Between the bitterness and advice seeking, I knew the stress of my job tormented and consumed me. I felt like a broken record facing the same issues, and I did not enjoy the person I was becoming.

A friend of mine asked me, "What is the common denominator in all these situations?" I left there pondering what she'd said, unsettled by the implication that the problem might be me. The thought irritated me at first, but beneath that resistance, a quiet realization stirred—perhaps there was something I needed to face, something I had been avoiding. As the saying goes, *"truth hurts."*

In September of that year, God kept talking to me as I continued reading Stormie Omartian's devotional *The Power of a Praying Woman.* I heard an audible voice say, "Quit your job and pursue your accounting business." I was confused, but then I heard, "Are you going to trust Me, give up control, and follow Me?" A few days later, I heard Him again: "Are you going to step out in obedience? I will provide more than you can ever fathom. All you have to do is trust and follow Me." Pursuing my own accounting business terrified me. I felt trapped between fear and faith, knowing obedience required movement even when safety begged me to stay still.

I mulled over what I felt God was saying to me for so long. I knew the direction to take, yet fear crippled me. Can you relate? Have you ever allowed fear to cripple you, even when you know God is directing your steps?

That fall, I turned forty and made up my mind. I knew I had to be obedient to what God asked of me. So I decided to quit my job and step into the unknown. I chose to pursue my accounting business full-time, essentially giving up all control of my financial stability. Executing this decision scared me. It felt like jumping off a cliff into nothingness. I am a planner and a controller. I know exactly how life will be—events, plans, and activities are marked down months in advance, and I know how much money is coming in and how much is going out. Sure, I had a few clients and ideas lined up, but I did not believe in myself, my worth, or my capability to be a successful entrepreneur. Fear had its grip on me and squeezed tightly.

Little did I know, that fear started an internal healing process I didn't see coming. When I decided to go on my own, I remember telling Dave, "I have no idea what I've done. We could go into a big hole financially, but this is a spiritual journey, and I need to be obedient." He looked at me and said, "I can live cheap; you, on the other hand, may need to change some of your habits." As I thought about it, he wasn't wrong; I don't live extravagantly by any means, but I will agree that I like to live comfortably.

A few weeks passed, and I finally mustered up the courage and gave notice to my employer. In the weeks leading up to this, I'd felt as if I had a huge rock on top of me, weighing me down. As soon as I gave my notice, I felt incredible relief—as if I could truly breathe for the first time in a long time. It was shocking! Mentally checked out of my job by this time, I didn't have the same concern about work as I had previously. I trained two people to take my place, a reality that made it unmistakably clear how hard I had worked for acceptance, validation, and worth in that position.

December 17, 2021, was my last day of work, and as as I drove home, the floodgates opened and tears flowed. I mourned the loss of the job, almost as if a death had occurred. So many feelings stirred in the coming days. I'd worked so hard to be acknowledged, accepted, and appreciated in those ten years of my life, and now it all seemed for naught. The life lessons were there for sure, and I had gained priceless business knowledge, but the heartache of feeling mistreated, stepped on, and overlooked left me feeling hopeless. Depression began to set in.

During December, I cancelled several get-togethers. I could not bring myself to be around people. I felt sad and cried a lot of the time. For the next few weeks, I did not want to get out of bed most days. I felt numb inside as if there was nothing to live for, and I felt I had single-handedly destroyed my life. What hurt even more was the loneliness. I felt invisible, overlooked, and unimportant. I felt that if I died, no one would even notice my absence. Without question, I didn't understand or know how to deal with all the emotions swirling at once.

I recall talking to my sister-in-law about how I felt. She shared that I showed signs of depression and cautioned me to watch for progression and to seek medical help. The onset of depression was difficult for me to understand. Having been raised in a small Manitoba community where mental illness was misunderstood and rarely spoken about didn't help matters. Growing up in such an atmosphere shaped my thinking.

I became fearful and began to believe there was something defective about me.

As the New Year rang in, I was searching for a fresh start. I set a New Year's resolution to get healthy in every way possible. This meant spiritually, mentally, emotionally, and physically. In January, I took a timeout and focused on just that. I figured there was no better way to start the year than by cleansing myself with the Daniel Fast, covering all aspects of my health. I had a friend who was willing to undertake the task with me, so we supported each other. I did not know if I would be able to complete it because part of the Daniel Fast is cutting out caffeine. Now, let's be honest, who can live without caffeine?

To my surprise, on day ten, I could feel the darkness lift from my mind. Not once had I focused all my worries into prayer before, nor had I fasted according to what this plan required. I learned a valuable lesson through this fast—to rely on prayer and God solely, which I had not truly done up to that point. I had a list of specific prayers I prayed daily. First and foremost, I prayed for my health to be restored spiritually, mentally, emotionally, and physically. Second, I prayed I would be able to believe in myself. And, finally, I prayed to have the wisdom to run my accounting business successfully. I stand amazed at how God worked in my life and how my mindset and circumstances were transformed. I definitely felt more focused and positive. I grew in my character, experienced mental clarity, and truly felt restored. I am so grateful for this life lesson, and it appeared to be the stepping stone to turning my self-esteem around.

Through my journey, I've learned that my root of obedience goes hand in hand with listening. Now, when I hear God speak to me or convict me, I step out in obedience no matter the cost. Unfortunately, this has meant dealing with things I wish I did not have to, such as anxiety, depression, trauma, emotions, slander, attacks on my integrity and my beliefs, and my anger.

Being obedient is not an effortless task, yet it is a very rewarding one. I know firsthand that God uses our obedience to Him to consistently grow our character. For this to come to fruition, I had to be willing, have an open mind and heart, and be in the right relationship with Him. I had to have courage, be open to new things, and persevere in the worst of times. Stormie Omartian tells us there is a direct connection between obedience and getting your prayers answered. Don't keep telling God what you want without asking Him what He wants.[9]

A scripture I would refer back to when I felt weary and needed hope is James 1: 2–8 (NLT):

Dear brothers and sisters, when troubles of any kind come your way, consider it an opportunity for great joy. For you know that when your faith is tested, your endurance has a chance to grow. So let it grow, for when your endurance is fully developed, you will be perfect and complete, needing nothing. If you need wisdom, ask your generous God, and he will give it to you. He will not rebuke you for asking. But when you ask him, be sure that your faith is in God alone. Do not waver, for a person with divided loyalty is as unsettled as a wave of the sea that is blown and tossed by the wind. Such people should not expect to receive anything from the Lord. Their loyalty is divided between God and the world, and they are unstable in everything they do.

When I felt lost, I would often seek God for wisdom and guidance. I asked questions such as, *Why is this happening to me? Why am I feeling this way? Why am I being treated so unfairly? What are you trying to teach me? Why me? I have done what you have asked of me; why am I still not healed?* Quite often He would answer me very clearly, providing insight for my life lesson and personal growth. However, there were also several times when I felt as if my prayers were unheard and the suffering would not end. Of course, the suffering did end, usually when I chose to be obedient.

Being obedient often means accepting change. Change is scary, and sometimes I am hesitant to step into change because I know what God is asking and the cost. Even as I am pushed beyond my limits and stretched in all aspects, I have to be willing to surrender, and surrender is something I have wrestled with for most of my life. Surrendering our human will is tough but doable. By leaning on God, I have learned to see things differently and ask Him to help me see situations through His eyes so I can respond accordingly.

Working on my root of obedience has broadened my horizon to blessings I could not have imagined. For things to fall into place, I had to be open to seeing life from a new perspective. I would often resist and stay stuck because where I stood provided comfort. I have learned to ask myself, "If I am comfortable, am I being obedient?" I am not saying we should by no means feel comfort or have times to come up for air, because I certainly did. But our comfort should come from trusting God regardless of the circumstances and into the next challenge and adventure God has planned for us.

Being obedient can hurt when you're trying to be a positive influence and the rejection remains consistent. It is painful and upsetting to face constant roadblocks and dead ends despite all your perseverance, knowledge, growth, and efforts. Sometimes following God's plan may be painful, as captured in Paul's obedience while anchored in surrender. Acts 20:22–24 (NLT) declares,

> *And now I am bound by the Spirit to go to Jerusalem. I don't know what awaits me, except that the Holy Spirit tells me in city after city that jail and suffering lie ahead. But my life is worth nothing to me unless I use it for finishing the work assigned me by the Lord Jesus—the work of telling others the Good News about the wonderful grace of God.*

Revelation 14:12 (NLT) confirms that we all may face suffering.

> *This means that God's holy people must endure persecution patiently, obeying his commands and maintaining their faith in Jesus.*

It takes courage and resilience to push onward when we feel like giving up. Just when I believed God had refined me and pruned this branch enough, He was at work once more as the process of surrendering started all over. He asked me to continue in obedience and work on more internal scars. Sometimes, I feel as if the last four years of my life have been full of nothing but pruning, refining, challenges, and roadblocks.

I read a powerful reminder by Stormie Omartian of what God requires from me and felt it described my journey. She states, "We can study all we want in His holy manual of life and learn everything we are supposed to do, but at some point we still have to jump in the water. The proof of our sincerity is in the doing, not just the knowing. Obedience is something you do; having a heart to obey is something you pray and ask God to give you."[10]

Talking about jumping into the water, one Sunday while I sat in church service, the children's ministry leader requested volunteers for the children's ministry as they were understaffed. I am not the most patient person, especially with a group of young children; however, I felt the nudge of God telling me to step out of the boat and get in the water. I needed to trust Him. Reluctantly, I decided to be obedient and raised my hand, offering to help. I fully trusted that God would walk with me through this new endeavor because I had no idea how to deal with this many kids. To my amazement, I really enjoyed helping the children learn about God. In fact, I've enjoyed it so much that I'm still in children's ministry but teaching older children. I've created bonds with some of the children and look forward to guiding them. Adults can genuinely learn so much from a child.

My journey has not been a bed of roses. It has left me weary, pondering my actions several times; however, it has also been very rewarding to watch myself be stretched beyond anything I ever imagined. Who knew that being obedient to His calling would require writing this book—an accountant-turned-author! A verse I try to live by is Philippians 4:9 (NIV), Paul writes,

> *Whatever you have learned or received or heard from me, or seen in me—put it into practice. And the God of peace will be with you.*

During a Bemer training event I attended, Ben Woodward, reminded me that "the valley of despair is not optional. It is a necessary part of the journey. The difference between those who succeed and those who fail is their ability to push through it."[11]

I encourage you to reflect on the above quotation and its relevance in your life. Reflect on your past and current circumstances. Are you willing to join me in pushing through and embracing everything that comes with being obedient? We will be better for it; we *just* have to surrender and trust the process. Remember:

> God has great plans for you. He has important things He wants you to do. And He is preparing you for your destiny right now. But you have to take steps of obedience in order to get there. And you have to trust that He knows the way and won't hurt you in the process.[12]

God's ways may lead us through valleys, but His heart is never to harm us. He walks every step with us if we allow Him to. I wholeheartedly experienced this while facing my deep root of obedience and, as you'll see in the next chapter, in the root of forgiveness.

Please scan the QR code to listen to the songs that became my prayer while healing this root.

Chapter Three

FORGIVENESS

If we really want to love, we must learn how to forgive.

—Mother Teresa

Sometimes forgiveness feels daunting, and I reject what I know I should do. To forgive someone who has hurt me so deeply can feel impossible, but I have learned over time that with God, all things are possible.

I believe that until I can walk a mile in Christ's shoes and truly wrap my mind around what He went through for my sins, I will never comprehend what forgiveness means on this side of heaven.

An excerpt from Stormie Omartian opened my eyes to the power of forgiveness.

> Often we don't recognize the unforgiveness that is in us.
> We think we are forgiving, but we really aren't. If we don't
> ask God to reveal our unforgiveness to us, we may never
> get free of the paralyzing grip it has on our lives. A big part
> of making sure our lives are clean and right before God
> has to do with forgiving other people. We can never move
> into all God has for us unless we do.[13]

Have you ever felt as if *you* were wronged? I know this may seem like a silly question, but several times in my life, I felt like a victim, and I could not forgive until I received a sincere apology. Does this resonate with you? Unfortunately, by stewing on a "wrong" and making a mountain out of a molehill, I dug myself a deeper pit of despair. At times, I harboured bitterness or resentment toward certain individuals as I longed to receive an apology. More often than not, these apologies did not come.

Eventually, I *thought* I had forgiven—or at least that is what I told myself so I could move on. But through my healing journey, I realized you can appear to forgive on the outside while still demanding accountability on the inside. In truth, that isn't forgiveness at all. There were times I said the words "I forgive you" when deep within my soul, I had not. I believed I deserved better. I believed I was right. But I had to learn what it meant to truly forgive from the inside out—a process which was both unique and profoundly transformative.

It is easy to fall into Satan's trap of unforgiveness when we have been wounded. Satan knows how to twist our feelings, feeding our pain and pride until bitterness and resentment take hold. When this happens, we open the door for him to have a foothold within our hearts.

Stormie Omartian reminded me that "when we forgive someone, it doesn't make them right or justify what they have done. It releases them into God's hands so He can deal with them. Forgiveness is undoubtedly the best revenge because it not only sets us free from the person we forgive, but it frees us to move into all God has for us."[14]

The day God spoke to me regarding forgiveness will forever be remembered as a reference point for my faith. Reading through *Overcoming Emotions*, I felt as if a knife had stabbed me in the heart and sliced it open. I started to cry, undone in a way I had not anticipated. I felt completely shattered as I realized how my actions with anger, disobedience, unforgiveness, and control all affected Christ. I wept for hours as I continued to read through the book, wiping my tears away as I turned the pages. I grieved for all the spears I thrust in Christ's side. Devastated, my eyes were swollen, and shame started to set in. Embarrassed by my behavior, actions, and thoughts, I didn't even know how to repent. I felt like a failure, unworthy, and thought how dare I ask God for anything when I can't follow a simple command about forgiveness. I grew up in the church with faith as a constant companion, yet I struggled to live out what God asked of me. This became a lightbulb moment as I started to dig out even more root issues.

During my quiet time, as I read Matthew 6:14–15 (NLT), the pain sank deeper. Jesus says,

> *"If you forgive those who sin against you, your heavenly Father will forgive you. But if you refuse to forgive others, your Father will not forgive your sins."*

Undeniably, because I held unforgiveness, God would not forgive me. It only makes sense; I mean, why would He? Sometimes I think we are all like this. We want to have a quick way out and expect forgiveness to be given to us while we refuse to forgive others. Why am I like this? I believe it happens because I feel entitled; I feel justified; I feel I deserve better. Each is a lie the enemy uses to blind us to the truth. We have to change the lens we're looking through and think with a new perspective. This journey taught me to surrender my sinful desires so God could work in and through me.

The powerful words in Stormie's desk calendar got my attention once again:

> God wants you to move into all He has for you. But if you don't forgive, you get stuck where you are and shut off God's work in your life. Forgiveness opens your heart and mind and allows the Holy Spirit to work freely in you. It releases you to love God more and discern His love in greater measure. Life is worth nothing without that.[15]

One day, while studying Scripture, I came across Christ's words in Mark 11:24–25 (NLT),

> *I tell you, you can pray for anything, and if you believe that you've received it, it will be yours. But when you are praying, first forgive anyone you are holding a grudge against, so that your Father in heaven will forgive your sins, too.*

Even though I had read that passage before, until that moment, it had not penetrated my heart the way it did on this healing journey. *I would not be forgiven because of my unwillingness to forgive others.* This stopped me in my tracks. Christ shares that not only are we to forgive, but we are also to forgive often. Matthew 18:21–22 (NIV) states:

> *Then Peter came to Jesus and asked, "Lord, how many times shall I forgive my brother or sister who sins against me? Up to seven times?" Jesus answered, "I tell you, not seven times, but seventy-seven times."*

I had a hard time coming to terms with this directive. How on God's green earth am I supposed to forgive someone seventy-seven times for the same thing? My human side would stand ground and push back, defending my rights, I can tell you that much!

Letting go of what I thought were "my rights" felt unfair. It made me feel like a doormat, and for a long time, I resisted. I began praying for God to uphold me and to change my heart because what He asked felt humanly impossible. I knew in my heart I could do all things through Christ according to His purpose, and I believe anything is possible—but this? This felt impossible. I understood God was not trying to take something from me—He was trying to free me from its weight. He wanted me to seek Him so I could continue to be transformed from the inside out. I had to learn to rely on Him completely so I could live out my faith in every area of my life, including this deep root of forgiveness.

Another challenging task came when the Holy Spirit directed me to sit face-to-face with Karsyn, someone who had deeply offended me. A word of caution: God required this of *me*. This may not be what He requires of you. Be attentive to His prompting and trust how He leads your heart. I needed to ask for forgiveness from her for my actions.

I lingered in that moment, before I went to see Karsyn, turning over the whole situation in my mind. I didn't know how to accomplish what He'd asked of me. I felt very raw but decided I needed to be faithful. God showed me that vulnerability was not optional—it was required. We cannot truly forgive if we are not vulnerable because forgiveness and vulnerability go hand in hand, whether it is given or received.

That's not a place I enjoy sitting. I don't know about you, but I don't like to show weakness or that I'm hurting, I messed up, or I don't have it all together, but that's what God asked me to reveal. He wanted me to openly share my unresolved hurt and struggle so she could understand I am a work in progress and see the changes that were starting to transform me. It took an immense amount of humility to obey. I knew being vulnerable would make me uncomfortable—a feeling so foreign that I actually felt sheepish and exposed even thinking about it. I did not know how to proceed and simply fell on my knees in prayer, begging God to give me the words to speak.

As I sank into the chair across from Karsyn, I ended up hyperventilating, trying to catch my breath as I started sharing the deep pain within me and the reason for this meeting. I did not know how to say what I came to say. I felt as if I were giving a painful birth to breech emotions. As I tried, my body started shaking. Karsyn placed her hand on mine, trying to calm and reassure me, and I could see the concern in her eyes—true, genuine concern for what I shared—as she had not seen this side of me. I'm pretty sure I blindsided Karsyn because I sure blindsided myself!

Eventually, I finally said everything I needed to say, and our friendship healed. That moment marked something deeper. I promised Karsyn I would seek help to truly heal. I started praying for God to open my eyes and to reveal where I needed to start so I could become who He wanted me to be. I became determined to truly heal, no matter the cost. As I left her home, I felt completely raw. My emotional pain reached depths I had not touched before, as God exposed the buried roots of unforgiveness. It became evident that forgiveness demanded I release what I had clung to for survival—my perception of safety: control, perfectionism, and trust in the wrong people.

I have come to realize that I hold my pain and emotions deep in my body—all part of the survival skills I mentioned in chapter one. As emotions release from my body, the process is excruciating—physically painful and mentally and emotionally exhausting.

I wasn't done yet, though. *Sigh.*

The same day, I had to share openly with my husband. In our entire life together, I had never shared these deep historic hurts with him. They were situations I had refused to talk about as I sought to protect myself and move forward. Never looking back.

Round two was on the horizon. I started sharing with my husband even deeper hurts God had revealed. I also had to ask Dave for forgiveness in many areas. As in any marriage, we had ups and downs our whole life together, but after he heard what I had to say, he sat there in disbelief. He had no idea I had endured so much pain and heartache. He knew my family and some stories but not as much as I shared with him at that moment. As I sobbed uncontrollably, he just held me as the floodgates opened. He witnessed the consequences of the pain I had held inside all those years. For me to be that vulnerable with anyone was nothing short of a miracle. Some of those memories I would have taken to my grave, but God had other plans and wanted them uncovered. Through this experience, I died to myself so I could become a new creation. Just as Paul writes in 2 Corinthians 5:17 (NIV),

> *Therefore, if anyone is in Christ, the new creation has come:*
> *The old has gone, the new is here!*

After I completed the massive task of sharing my deep hurts, I begged God for a break. I could hardly function and needed to heal from what had just transpired. I cried on and off all day, and at no point in my life had I ever felt so exposed.

The next day, Sunday morning, as I sat in church, I wept through the sermon. The Holy Spirit hit me hard with exactly what I needed to hear. The praise and worship songs penetrated deep into my soul as I tried to sing amid the brokenness. I experienced true transformation for the first time. The pastor had handed out sticky notes for specific prayer requests to be brought to the front and placed on the cross. I thought, *Where do I start?* So I asked for healing, to be restored in every aspect, and for strength. My loving husband brought the notes to the front and stuck them on the cross for me as I could not bear the thought of walking to the altar in front of everyone.

As time passed, I did heal and became stronger in my faith. I thought God might be done with the refining process, and I could sense my faith stretching to new depths. Excitement stirred as I thought about what lay ahead.

Then, once again, God showed up.

A specific person came to the forefront of my mind, and the Holy Spirit told me in an audible voice to ask for her forgiveness. I had not spoken to this person in a long while, and our falling out had taken place twenty-four years prior. God prompted me to reach out to apologize for my behavior. He made the wounds and my actions very clear to me during this time, and I deeply regretted the hurt my negative emotions inflicted on her so many years before.

As I asked for this person's forgiveness, I suddenly realized that I had done something I'd sworn I would never do to a friend—and I had done it to the truest friend I'd ever had. She listened as I wailed over the phone, and then she reassured me that she had forgiven me a long time ago. In the past, I had buried the hurt and walked away, retreating into survival mode instead of dealing with my hurt the way Christ wanted me to. God worked to prune me, and in the process, He restored my long-lost friendship. Even when I could not see His plans, He knew what I needed.

Unfortunately, on the evening of January 12, 2023, a driver slammed into my stopped vehicle as I waited to merge onto a busy highway. I was positioned to merge, with my body completely twisted to the left, leaned forward and lifted off the seat while checking over my shoulder, essentially looking behind me at the time of impact. This left me with a tremendous amount of injury. I suffered from a full-body whiplash, a rotator cuff injury on my right shoulder, a painful nerve sensation running down my arm, nerve pain in my right foot, a bone jarred on top of my right foot, and soft tissue damage to the inside of my right ankle—all of which hindered me from walking. Even more, I suffered from an injury in my neck, nerve pain down the left side of my body, scar tissue on the left side of my lower back, and major discomfort, muscle injury, and inflammation. These experiences and traumas are parts of my life I would love to forget. The deep trauma I encountered and the constant struggle I faced became a tough battle. I could no longer walk—at least not well, and sometimes not at all. If I did walk, it felt as if sharp, jagged stones were ripping the muscles or tendons from the bottom of my right foot. To function through the excruciating pain, I took prescribed medication daily.

As the inflammation in my back settled down, I saw a physiotherapist. When she used intramuscular stimulation (IMS) needling on me, my body flared up severely, causing a worse state of pain than before I went to see her.

Two days after the IMS needling, on March 12, 2023, misfortune struck again with another accident. This time I was hit from the front, and as I saw it coming, I braced for impact. In hindsight, that was the worst thing I could have done for my body. I can still hear the sound of the crushing metal, a sound I did not know would affect me adversely in the months to come. I felt completely fractured emotionally, angry at the people who hit me, and in so much pain that the pharmaceutical medications hardly touched it. I had a hard time standing and sitting due to muscle and nerve pain, and on several days I was forced into bed before 6:30 p.m. Functioning in any situation seemed to be a challenge.

As the days passed, I found myself on edge and angry at pretty much everything and everyone. The physical destruction my body experienced caused me to self-destruct. I felt alone, and it frustrated me that I could not function. My mind wanted to accomplish things my body could not. I remained stuck, unable to cope, as the people around me continued with life as though nothing had happened. Unfortunately, this took a toll on my mental state, as anyone who goes through chronic pain can attest.

It did not enter my thoughts to forgive those who had caused me so much pain. Mentally, I struggled. If I saw them face-to-face, I wanted to inflict the amount of pain on them that they had caused me. Revenge stood at the forefront of my mind, even though I knew both collisions were apparently accidents.

As we discussed in Chapter 1, sometimes anger is my response to deep hurts, my way of covering up emotions. I don't want to deal with the deeper issue. Living through the horrible pain that I endured was rough. Separating what happened from the understanding that the other drivers didn't intentionally hurt me felt impossible. I felt that they should have known better. They could have looked more carefully, they could have paid attention, but they didn't—and yet they got off scot-free. I could not even walk, but these individuals carried on with life as though nothing had happened, and that made me even angrier every time I thought about it. *This is not fair. Why me?*

There appeared to be a link between the pain I endured and the fact that men were causing it. A man inflicted the trauma in my childhood; these two separate accidents were caused by male drivers. I started to insert a barrier in my mind, associating men with pain and trauma. Needless to say, this was not a great mindset to apply in my marriage, and my emotions were in disarray.

It's only by the grace of God that I forgave these drivers, because in my heart, I'm not sure I could have on my own. My human nature finds it almost impossible to forgive someone when I am hurting and suffering so deeply. After reading Ephesians 4:31–32 (NIV), I eventually came to terms, and I truly forgave these men as God commands: "Get rid of all bitterness, rage and anger, brawling and slander, along with every form of malice. Be kind and compassionate to one another, forgiving each other, just as in Christ God forgave you." I find there is nothing more eye-opening than reading Scripture and finding the answer to an issue I am facing. God always finds a way to speak to me. As I mentioned earlier, He will use anything to get my attention, and then I know what is required. Whether I want or agree with what He requires is a totally different matter!

Everything I went through up to this point had a purpose for my spiritual growth, even though I could not recognize it at the time. Life's lessons were attached to the events I had faced, some more painful than others. If we don't forgive, we are simply punishing ourselves. Forgiveness is not about the other person; it is about *us* and setting ourselves free. I did not want the unforgiveness to consume my thoughts and actions anymore. I did not want Satan to have a foothold in my heart. I did not want to be held in bondage or shackled with chains. We can in no way be who God intends us to be if we are hanging on to bitterness, resentment, and unforgiveness. If I had chosen to stay where I was, I would not be where I am today.

To truly forgive, try to envision yourself in Christ's shoes as He endured the brutal suffering on the cross. With this imagery in my mind, I reflected on the times I've prayed for God to forgive me, and things were brought into perspective pretty quickly, especially when I recalled how many times I specifically prayed for forgiveness for my anger. I wept uncontrollably as I envisioned a lashing on Christ's body for my sin. Every time I needed to be forgiven, Christ bore my punishment. That's a pretty sobering thought in the big scheme of things. How dare I not pass forgiveness on to others after what Christ endured for me? Using this visualization technique shifted the lens through which I saw forgiveness, and I viewed my actions in a whole new way. At the core of forgiveness is a repentant heart.

The most impactful weapon I had was prayer. Through prayer, I felt God's presence, and I began to see things through His eyes. Prayer helped to strengthen my heart and mind and allowed me to show Christ's love and compassion in all circumstances. He kept pouring wisdom into me through scripture. Ephesians 4:1–3 (NIV) states:

> *As a prisoner for the Lord, then, I urge you to live a*
> *life worthy of the calling you have received. Be completely*

> *humble and gentle; be patient, bearing with one another in love. Make every effort to keep the unity of the Spirit through the bond of peace.*

Too often, we worry about what lies ahead and allow our thoughts to spiral into anxiety and anger. We have to hand everything over to God in prayer. Some things are not ours to carry. God knew my heart and the antidote I needed for complete restoration, and He alone could overhaul my heart. During this overhaul, my roots were exposed as He brought them to the surface so I could process them.

As we live out our faith, let's heed this word of caution: don't become idle, thinking we have "fire insurance." Satan works hard at destroying what God created, and my prayer is that we will all reflect on the seriousness of 2 Peter 2:20–21 (NIV):

> *If [we] have escaped the corruption of the world by knowing our Lord and Savior Jesus Christ and are again entangled in it and are overcome, [we] are worse off at the end than [we] were at the beginning. It would have been better for [us] not to have known the way of righteousness, than to have known it and then to turn [our] backs on the sacred command that was passed on to [us].*

In Scripture, God shows a way for all of us to combat the "devil's schemes." I believe this is the most important passage for a Christian to know how to protect what God has created. The passage in Ephesians 6:10–18 (NIV) is often referred to as "The Armour of God."

Finally, be strong in the Lord and in his mighty power. Put on the full armor of God, so that you can take your stand against the devil's schemes. For our struggle is not against flesh and blood, but against the rulers, against the authorities, against the powers of this dark world and against the spiritual forces of evil in the heavenly realms. Therefore put on the full armor of God, so that when the day of evil comes, you may be able to stand your ground, and after you have done everything, to stand. Stand firm then, with the belt of truth buckled around your waist, with the breastplate of righteousness in place, and with your feet fitted with the readiness that comes from the gospel of peace. In addition to all this, take up the shield of faith, with which you can extinguish all the flaming arrows of the evil one. Take the helmet of salvation and the sword of the Spirit, which is the word of God. And pray in the Spirit on all occasions with all kinds of prayers and requests. With this in mind, be alert and always keep on praying for all the Lord's people.

I share this passage because I believe in my heart and soul that unforgiveness is where Satan traps much of his prey. Unforgiveness may feel justified, but spiritually, it becomes an opening the enemy eagerly exploits. What we refuse to release, he uses to keep us bound. Forgiveness is not weakness. It is warfare. When we forgive, we shut the door to the enemy, restore our armor, and reclaim our position in Christ. Freedom begins the moment we choose to lay down what was never meant to be carried.

Satan would have liked nothing better than for me to harbour all the unforgiveness I had in my heart. Satan is conniving and sneaky and comes in under the radar when we least expect it. I did not know, until my healing process began, that I had allowed Satan to have a foothold in my heart through unforgiveness. 1 Peter 5:8–9 (NIV) cautions us to "be alert and of sober mind. Your enemy the devil prowls around like a roaring lion looking for someone to devour. Resist him, standing firm in the faith, because you know that the family of believers throughout the world is undergoing the same kind of sufferings." To combat the devil and all his schemes, we have to faithfully use "The Armour of God."

> If you can think of someone whom you find it hard to forgive, ask God to give you a heart of forgiveness for them. Pray for them in all the ways you can think of to pray. It's astonishing how God softens our hearts when we pray for people. Our anger, resentment, and hurt turn into love.[16]

In releasing unforgiveness, I uncovered a deeper truth: control had been my silent companion all along.

Please scan the QR code to explore the songs that impacted my soul during this season.

Chapter Four

CONTROL

When everything seems to be going against you, remember that the airplane takes off against the wind, not with it.

—Henry Ford

As the physical pain continued to plague my body, weariness set in. I could not enjoy even minor activities with my daughter or perform simple tasks such as getting dressed, moving freely, buying groceries, cooking, etcetera. After struggling for a few weeks, unable to work, I felt defeated, lost, and often hopeless. I found it extremely difficult to sit still and not be productive or in control of what was happening to me.

After I had endured months of suffering, a friend of mine mentioned a medical device from Europe that could help me. As I began using the device, my body started changing. I began my own research study to better understand what happened before, during, and after using the device. I also found three willing participants who happened to be at my house at the time. Intrigued by the progress they saw in me and curious about what this device might do for their own ailments, my mother, stepdad, and husband all agreed to let me track their progress.

On day two of using the device, I regained eighty percent of the use of my right arm, which got my attention. In the days leading up to this, I could hardly hold a coffee cup up to my mouth with my right arm. I had to tuck my arm right by my side in order to function with it at all. Intrigued and curious about this seemingly magical device, I kept digging into the research behind it. I needed to comprehend how and why it worked and what was taking place to cause such rapid healing. What I discovered made complete sense, and it fundamentally brought me back to how God created me.

By day five, the pain had lifted from my back. I felt completely healed and stood amazed as if a miracle had happened in my body. I recall telling my husband, "I could do cartwheels and run a marathon. I feel good. I'm healed." He looked at me and said, "Whoa, whoa, whoa! Back up! What's going on?!" As I explained further every detail of what I felt, we both looked at each other in amazement. Unless you've lived in terrible pain and experienced firsthand the dramatic relief this medical device provides, it is impossible to fully understand what I am trying to describe.

Most importantly, on day five, I heard the Holy Spirit speak to me. He told me in an audible voice, "This is the miracle for your friend and brother." I stood in disbelief, trying to wrap my head around what I had just heard from the Holy Spirit. The device would become a gift to heal my friend, who at the time faced a terminal diagnosis. Her body continued to fail her, and the prognosis looked grim. Up until this time, I had prayed for three years for my friend to be healed, that God would lay his hands on her and heal her from the inside out. Well, this friend proved to be another miracle before my eyes, and the device did exactly what God said it would! I experienced pure joy as I watched her regain her health.

Shortly after witnessing this miracle, while driving home from a visit with my friend, it dawned on me that this medical device had accomplished exactly what I'd prayed for. I had watched my prayers come to life—word for word—right before my eyes. As the realization set in, I bawled. My heart overflowed with gratitude. God had answered my prayers, but never in my wildest dreams had I ever thought it would happen this way. I could not wrap my mind around how God worked and what He provides. I had to endure months of agony to discover a device that could save my friend's life. This felt like a dream—as if someone needed to pinch me and wake me up. It just didn't feel real, but I sure celebrated!

The day I witnessed this miracle became the day I started a new business. I became an independent distributor for the medical device company, and God started using me to impact others' lives—not only with the healing He was providing through this device but also by allowing me to witness to people's spirits. I openly share my day-five experience and what I heard the Holy Spirit say to me when I talk about what this device has done for me. Some people may look at me sideways and wonder about the state of my mind, but it doesn't stop me because I'm here for a higher purpose. Everyone God has brought into my path since this new endeavor, He has placed there for a reason. Whether I am an inspiration to them, an encouragement, or a bringer of hope, He has a purpose for why I have met them. I have a new confidence in my faith due to this impact and openly declare my faith to others. It did not take long for me to sense that the team members I was working with in the device company were Christ followers, ones who share my faith and with whom I can openly discuss my faith. I sense that God has a plan I can't yet fathom.

Even though my body had transformed greatly, at this point, I still suffered from nerve injury on the left side of my body and right foot, which left me unable to walk. With the exception of the middle of my back, the rest of my body seemed to be healing fine. However, there were setbacks ahead in my healing. Healing is indisputably a slow process and one you need patience for when nerves are involved.

During June 2023, I took a trip back to Manitoba to visit family. I tried to "suck it up" and make the best of my days, yet I was unable to control the pain while walking. The nerve pain in my left leg became so intense that it drove me to my wits' end. I found myself trapped in a relentless cycle—moving to ease the nerve pain on the left side of my body while enduring immense pain in my right foot. The lack of control became overwhelming.

I am sure my family and friends can attest that I did not resemble my normal self. And honestly, who could while living with relentless nerve pain? I did not want to become a broken record, constantly voicing how deeply the pain affected me. So instead, I tried to bury it and carry on. Looking back, I recognize that I did not always succeed. My mind struggled to track conversations, drifting instead toward one consuming question: *How am I going to make it through the day?* To some, it may have appeared that I had checked out, and I believe there is truth to that.

Unless you have walked a mile in my shoes, it's hard to understand the agony I faced while simply trying to function.

Near the end of the trip to Manitoba, believing I still had some control over what was happening in my body, I decided to go see a "nerve guy" whom people claimed was a miracle worker. He came highly recommended by those close to me. I trusted my family and friends and figured maybe this "nerve guy" could figure out the problem in my foot and left leg so I could finally walk pain-free. After all, the nerve pain had worn me down—especially the inability to walk properly or for any distance. I booked the appointment with excitement stirring as I thought this might be my answer. Boy, was I mistaken!

The visit lasted forty-five minutes and is a memory I wish I could erase. I cried out in pain as this individual used excessive force on my poor body. My muscles and tendons were taking a beating, and I questioned him about what he was doing. He said I needed to endure the pain so things could get reset. He worked on everything from the scalenes in my neck to my ribs, vertebrae in my back, my pelvis, and my hips. I made sure he knew everything in my history regarding the accidents and how my body became mangled. The amount of pain I endured during this visit was bloody torture. I felt held hostage, deliberately harmed with excessive force. At one point, I wanted to yell, "Stop!" I could not bear it anymore, but in my mind, I heard a common phrase: *No pain, no gain.* I wondered about stopping; if he had only completed half the work, what would it mean for my body?

Regrettably, I pressed on, forcing myself to endure what felt like endless torture. In between the tears, I caught my breath while begging God to take the pain from me. I felt crushed in my spirit and in my heart. This took pain to an entirely new level. I walked into the session willingly, anchored in trust with those closest to me. I expected a gentle healing session, something restorative. What I encountered instead dismantled that expectation. We were headed out of town, so my precious daughter came with me to the appointment. As a mother, I am supposed to protect my child, not expose her to the trauma of watching me suffer. I hurt on a new level, emotionally and physically, and now I was beyond furious at the so-called "nerve guy" and those who had recommended him to me.

Before my daughter and I left town, I stopped at a friend's house to say goodbye. She knew about my visit to the "nerve guy" and watched me struggle to walk as she welcomed us inside. The weight of emotional and physical pain drew tears down my cheeks. I didn't know how to cope with what had just unfolded.

I felt betrayed by those closest to me and knew that the physical pain and emotions I felt were consuming me. I knew in my heart my loved ones would not have recommended someone who would deliberately harm me, but that's what took place. Have you trusted advice given in love, only to be left reeling by the outcome? I did not know how to work through the hurricane of emotions I experienced. My misplaced trust left me standing in the wreckage, unsure how to make peace with the choice I had made.

As our visit continued, a third person joined us, and before I knew it, I found myself in what I equated to an intervention. The conversation shifted to how I constantly do too much for others, stretching myself too thin. My friend declared the added stress hindered my healing and that I needed to face my emotions head-on. At this point, overwhelm consumed me. After everything that had unfolded earlier, my mind could no longer process what anyone said. Survival narrowed my options—I defaulted to anger and defensiveness: my crutch and the only way to stay standing. I endured the attack, but my friend dismissed every effort I had made toward healing in an instant.

Betrayal cut deep, especially coming from those closest to me. I heard comments like, "She's an Eight—the Challenger—on the Enneagram, which is extremely different from you." The words landed without meaning; I had not even heard of the Enneagram before. I remained frozen, appearing present, but internally, I hid behind my brick wall. I could not take another blow. No one seemed to acknowledge what I had just endured, much less the pain that brought me to the "nerve guy" to begin with. The judgement added on top of my injury felt unbearable; they might as well have thrown me off a cliff and gotten it over with. I shut down completely, and every suggestion bounced off a wall I did not know how to lower. Functioning required everything I had. Trapped in survival mode, my only focus centered on how to cope long enough to make it through the day.

I know my body, and I embraced the uphill battle to repair what had been done. I mean, you can't just karate chop a person's pelvis into place when it's out over an inch. The pain in my back became so unbearable that I wished I had died that day so that I did not have to endure the suffering that persisted. I believe I have a high pain tolerance, but this pushed me beyond anything I had ever experienced. It was a level of agony I had no reference point for. Even childbirth with back labor paled in comparison to the state my body had reached.

In the midst of it all, I discovered skin missing on my back. The so-called "nerve guy" had used a wooden tool to force my body into position, leaving more than just pain behind. A scar now marks my back—a permanent reminder of what took place, one I will carry for the rest of my life. The realization that yet another man had caused me harm ignited something deeper within me. Perhaps you have felt this, too: a rage simmering beneath the surface, tangled with shock and disbelief. To this day, the appointment with the "nerve guy" is the greatest regret of my life.

Later that evening, I polished off a bottle of red wine, desperate to numb the pain in every way. Yes, I was taking prescription meds and consuming alcohol to numb what I felt; I self-medicated with anything I hoped would end my pain. I wanted to drown out the memory and erase the day from my life. I wanted the suffering to stop. Have you been brought to this point as well, where the lack of control is simply too great to bear?

The next morning, misery greeted me as I prepared to fly home. The appointment had caused a massive setback—every part of my body ached, and emotionally, I remained completely undone with no control over how I felt. I could not compartmentalize what had happened; my emotions spilled out freely. Anger sat front and center, demanding release, yet I felt trapped inside it with no clear way out.

For the next two weeks, I lived in a zero-gravity chair on my deck, staring out across the fields as my body tried to recover. Sitting upright for any length of time felt impossible, so the option to lie back became my only relief. As I gazed into the distance, waves of emotions overtook me. I sobbed frequently as anger turned inward. It felt as though my healing had been stripped back to square one, my body undone, and my medical device was pushed into overdrive just to help me survive.

I was furious with myself for listening to others. *I should have only trusted myself,* I kept thinking. Do you struggle with this self-reliant belief too? Here I thought this "nerve guy" would be the answer to help me walk, and instead I became a walking disaster. Once again, I found myself in the "valley." The progress I had fought so hard to gain control of vanished, and new symptoms surfaced—ones I had not faced during previous appointments. That season marked the beginning of something else entirely. Unbeknownst to me at the time, the symptoms of PTSD quietly entered the picture, layering emotional trauma on top of an already broken body.

While reading Stormie Omartian's daily calendar, I was reminded that "sometimes we don't forgive ourselves for things we've done, and so we give ourselves a lifetime of punishment for whatever we did or did not do. Sometimes we blame God for things that have happened. Ask God to show you if any of these things are true about you. Don't let unforgiveness limit what God wants to do in your life."[17] Stormie's words had me thinking. I wrestled for a long time to forgive myself and the "nerve guy" for this horrible experience. I wish I could say I hadn't, but I also blamed God for not answering my many prayers. For a long while, I abandoned prayer altogether. I could not see the point anymore. Have you ever felt abandoned in the very place where you were told hope should live? Sometimes it seems none of our prayers are answered the way we hoped, and the suffering shows no sign of letting up. *Why even pray?* I thought. *It's useless.*

I continued to spiral, and my frustration spilled out to those closest to me. If anger ever had the upper hand, it was during this season. A raw, unfamiliar rage surfaced—one I had not tapped into before. I clung to mantras to survive: *one hour at a time . . . one day at a time . . . tomorrow is a new day . . . this will pass.* Yet even with those reminders, I struggled to tolerate myself. Negativity and anger clung to me like a shadow, leaving me unrecognizable. I thought to myself, *Can I not catch a break? Do I really have to deal with this?* I cried, begged, and pleaded with God to take the pain away. I could not see a lesson in the suffering or understand why I had to endure what felt like an endless hell. I could not comprehend how I had been so wrong—how one appointment had altered the entire course of my recovery.

Throughout that summer, the absence of control weighed heavily as nerve pain raged relentlessly. I prayed for God to take me home. I had stopped asking why. I simply wanted the suffering to end. Perhaps you've known this place, too, where prayers shift from answers to release. If so, you are not alone.

In my search for relief, I came across Dr. Rob Reimer's book *Soul Care,* where he shares powerful wisdom on the root of control.

The Lie of Control

I am a classic type-A personality. An overachiever, driven, in-charge type of person. I want to control the outcome of the things I care about. If I work hard and produce good results, I feel good. But if I work hard and things don't come around, I can feel irritable and angry. What's underneath that? The issue of my value is somehow connected to my capacity to produce results and control the outcomes that I desire. And if I can't produce results, it diminishes my worth. That's not true, but there are times in my life I have acted on that lie—more times than I wish to recall. It leaves me feeling an internal pressure to produce results; it is a self-inflicted pressure that comes from standing on the faulty foundation. I have to get off the poor foundation to release that internal pressure in my soul. The stress and pressure I feel isn't the problem; it is simply a symptom that points me to the real problem—I am trying, in this moment, to build my life on a lie, and my soul knows it. People who have been abused often struggle with control issues. Fear is always lurking underneath the desire to be in control.[18]

This captured my experience perfectly. This wisdom gave me the insight I had been searching for and equipped me to finally begin processing the root of control in my life. These words affirmed that I was not flawed or broken; rather, my mindset had been shaped through what I had endured, and now I had permission and clarity to change it. And so do you!

That summer, I went to my doctor, desperate for answers as nerve pain stole my ability to walk comfortably. I asked for a referral to a foot specialist and pushed for a full spinal scan, convinced something physical had been damaged in the accidents. Instead, they denied me, stating nothing warranted further investigation and that I would likely need nerve medication for life. I left defeated, with no referrals, no scan, and prescriptions I had no intention of using—another blow to my recovery.

At the next visit, the doctor reprimanded me for not taking the medications properly. After a week with no improvement, I refused to keep swallowing pills meant to mask symptoms rather than address the source. I asked for a counselling referral, desperately needing support as everything spiraled out of control, only to learn insurance required a doctor's approval. Instead of support, she handed me a questionnaire for anxiety and depression, another pathway to medication. I left discouraged and alone, with no answers and no relief. It became clear that if I wanted healing, I would have to fight to discover the root of my pain myself.

On August 22, 2023, we left on our annual family vacation to Prince Rupert. I rode in the car with my medical device beside me, unable to sit for long without unbearable nerve pain. Seven months of pain and immobility had pushed me to the edge. I gazed out the window quietly, forcing a smile for my family while everything inside me churned. A violent storm of emotions raged inside me—ones I did not yet know how to process. Defeated on all fronts with no hope on the horizon, I struggled to be positive. I carried anger toward my doctor and anger toward God for allowing this torment. My anger raged beneath the surface, desperate for release. While my family carefully tiptoed those first days, they watched me unravel as I struggled to steady myself.

I had four hours in the car to pray and pour out my heart to God before we reached the town of Smithers. He already knew every thought I carried, but that did not stop me from unleashing them all. During that drive, God received the full fury of my heart—far more than anyone else ever had. I silently prayed the loudest prayers my soul could muster. Have you trusted God enough to give Him your fury, not just your faith? Have you found yourself in this place too? I will admit, I had not been this low before. But the low was about to go even lower.

We were headed to Terrace for the night and stopped at Lake Isle Provincial Park, drawn in by the water. Dave pulled into a different parking lot than I had planned, and though it was a small deviation, it immediately reminded me how little control I had over anything anymore. We saw a neat walkway and a salmon viewing platform near the river, so we decided to venture down the path. Although I moved slowly, I could see the salmon swimming upstream. They made it look easy, but my pain made everything harder. Despite my discomfort, it was a wonderful experience to witness.

As we continued down the winding path, it appeared we were headed to Grouchy's Beach. Normally, a beach is not far from the parking lot, and you can almost see it; however, this time, it was hidden deep in the woods. I had no idea how far we were headed, and with every step, my body betrayed me. I limped in pain, unable to judge my own limits. Dave could not remember the distance. We walked on the path for what seemed like an eternity to me, with still no sign of the beach. I asked repeatedly, "Where the heck is this beach? I can't go any further." I was growing irritated and hurting deeply when Dave answered, "It's got to be just around the corner." I kept rounding corners, waiting for a beach to appear—but it never did. We continued, but after what felt like fifteen endless minutes, I could not take it anymore. I had to turn back. In unbearable pain, I turned, limping toward the car, my foot throbbing, anger boiling over. I thought to myself, *This holiday sucks! This is not what I had envisioned.* I walked in front of my family on the trail, almost certain that they could see the steam coming through my ears. Hot under the collar, one thought consumed me: *Check the sign.* When I finally reached the parking lot, I saw it: *Grouchy's Beach: 900 meters.* I glared at Dave when he asked, "What, you can't walk 900 meters?" Something snapped. "You thought I could walk a kilometer in my condition?!" Fury stole my voice. This was not anger—it was disbelief. *How could the man I married be so blind to my pain?*

Words failed me, but sarcasm did not. "Now I know why they call it Grouchy's Beach," I announced. "You're grouchy by the time you get there!" That half-hour walk in my condition sidelined me for days. I could barely walk before, and now the pain defied description.

The next day, we finally made it to Prince Rupert and headed out for whale watching. As we waited on the pier for the boat, I hobbled past a quaint coffee shop that served lattes and fresh baked goods. The delicious smell wafted in the air, and I thought of having a fresh-baked muffin and a vanilla latte. For nearly eight years, I had stayed gluten-free because of the pain it caused my body—but that day, I threw in the towel. I had reached a place where pain felt limitless. What did it matter if I added more when I felt as though no more pain was possible?

As I enjoyed my blueberry crumble muffin from a bench on the pier while staring out over the water, Dave sauntered up and unwisely asked if I thought I should be eating the muffin. If looks could kill, he would be lying dead on the pier in Prince Rupert. Let's just say I set him straight with a colorful phrase and put him firmly in his place. After all, no one knew my pain or what gluten did to my body better than I did. The day unraveled quickly from there. Indignation took hold, and I could not shake his comment. Everything—lack of empathy, control, progress—spilled on top of me, burying me alive, stealing my breath. Each time I clawed my way up, something pulled me back down into a dark pit of torment.

My healing journey up to that point had been quite a roller coaster, and in the valleys, I struggled mightily. To be quite frank, I'm shocked we made it through that trip in one piece, including me and my husband and daughter.

As we headed home from Prince Rupert, I chose to release my grip. I began shifting my mindset, leaning into prayer again, and allowing God to meet me there. This time, not full of fury but full of grace and peace. As we surrender our will and lean on God, peace will begin to take hold. Surrendering can be very freeing if we allow space for it. The difference came when I stopped fighting and, without reservation, surrendered my will. For someone with a challenger spirit, relinquishing control is a hard battle to face. I did not realize how incapable I felt with control stripped away—how paralyzing it became. Letting go of control felt like death. Without it, my body panicked; as control had become my refuge, my armor, my version of safety. Looking back, I can see how deeply our childhood survival programming fuels our need to control every environment. Our brain equates control with safety.

Letting go of control means placing the reins of our lives in God's hands. We have to trust what will unfold, even though it often requires unlearning everything we once relied on, which I believe is ten times harder than learning something new. Dr. Rob Reimer shares powerfully once again:

> The good news is that your value is not determined by whether or not you are in control. Strengthening a faulty foundation only reinforces a doomed building. Your value is not determined by your performance or whether people love you or whether you are in control. These are all core lies that can create cracks in the foundation and

damage your soul. You need to replace them with the truth. The issue of your value is settled at the cross. This is the truth that you must hold on to. This is the truth that you must appropriate every time the lies threaten your security, value, and identity. This is what God has accomplished in your spirit, and what you must hold on to and work out in your soul. This is the foundation that you must build your life upon. Upon this foundation you can find peace, love, acceptance, security, significance, and all you need in life.[19]

Through *Soul Care*, God spoke to my soul in a mighty way. The answers were in front of me. I needed to focus on the truth, but how was that possible when my whole life I had I felt programmed to act a certain way? The process of unlearning was a daunting task and seemed to take forever. I have not perfected the task to this day; however, I have come leaps and bounds from where I once stood. I believe switching foundations will be a continual journey as long as I live. I simply remember and remind myself of the truth and of who I am in Christ. As Dr. Rob Reimer shares, our value was settled at the cross. When we can remember this and place the thought in the forefront of our minds, we will have better days. To get there, we have to change our mindset and our thinking, as the Apostle Paul declares in Romans 12:2 (NLT):

> *Don't copy the behavior and customs of this world, but let God transform you into a new person by changing the way you think. Then you will learn to know God's will for you, which is good and pleasing and perfect.*

When you feel let down or that you are not valued by others, you literally have to remind yourself, *God loves me; my value comes from God; my worth is in Christ; nothing else matters.* Essentially, give yourself a positive pep talk, reassuring yourself of your value. Oh, I know it is easy to stay stuck in the negative thinking pattern and go down the rabbit trail of a downward spiral. Trust me, I've lived there far too long. But for the first time, I am genuinely realizing my value comes from a powerful source, which is Christ.

Do you have an identity wound as I did? Dr. Rob Reimer shares an image that has impacted me ever since I first read his words.

> Think of your soul as a bucket. When you have an identity wound, it is like having a hole in the bottom of your bucket. No matter what gets poured into the bucket, it doesn't stick—it just leaks out the bottom. People with an identity wound can have an encounter with God's love, but the love leaks out. People say loving and kind things to them, but nothing sticks. They have to repair the hole in the bottom of the bucket. For example, growing up in a home in which parents are highly critical leaves a hole in a person's bucket. No matter what you did, it wasn't enough. You brought home four A's and one B on the report card, and you were criticized for the B—even if it was somewhat in jest. There was just no affirmation for the A's.... Sometimes the hole is formed because you grew up in a home where you were never told that you were loved; you were never affirmed and appropriately hugged

and touched. These kinds of identity wounds leave you with a feeling of toxic shame.[20]

All of a sudden, my life seemed to make sense. I connected that all my struggles with control were rooted in an "identity wound." Have you considered that you may have an identity wound? I was curious, so I chose to dig deeper. God stirred my heart like a hurricane, gaining speed. I became determined to confront the problem before me and to heal the wounds I carried. I also recognized that this same pattern had crept into my own family. As a reflection of my own unresolved pain, I often criticized my daughter.

A month before our family trip, while trying to get back on track with business, I flew to Medicine Hat, Alberta, with a coworker for training. This new adventure intrigued me. The sessions went far beyond business practices; they applied to anything you chose to pursue in life. For example, I came to understand the attitude I bring to relationships, how to navigate challenges and roadblocks, and how to overcome fear. My big takeaway was the "GPS concept." The GPS concept is best explained this way: when we hit a roadblock in life, we need to recalculate just as a GPS does in our car. We can choose to take an alternative approach.

The weekend turned out to be far more meaningful than I'd expected. Although it demanded deep self-reflection, I found the experience unexpectedly fulfilling. I distinctly recall sitting down with the corporate representative and articulating my vision for the product—and the concrete steps I planned to take to move it forward. She spoke with clarity and directness, yet somehow without provoking me—a rare skill, especially since confrontation often sends me into protection mode, ready to push back. With every response I gave, she would challenge me to provoke a deeper thought process. Not once had someone led me to think this way. She challenged me every step of the way with every thought and answer I gave. This was good even though it irritated me. I will unfailingly remember her last words to me. She said, "I know your issue, and if I tell you right now, I would mess up your makeup, so I'm not going to tell you, but when you're ready, get a hold of me." I could not move. I could barely breathe. *How on earth could a complete stranger know my issues?* It's not as if I had a sign on my forehead for the world to see!

As my friend and I left the training, I looked at her and said, "What the heck just happened?" It felt as though a giant billboard stood directly in front of me, leaving no room to look away from the root issues God had begun to reveal. My friend confirmed what stirred inside me and gently acknowledged the depth of emotional work still ahead. I sensed God drawing buried pain to the surface, I felt it rising within me, and in that moment, I knew there was no turning back. Have you ever recognized the moment when God invited you forward, even though turning back would have been easier? If so, don't hold back—this is often where healing quietly begins.

Traveling home from this event, I began to grasp how profoundly these lessons applied to my personal life. I reflected deeply on everything I had learned. Curious, I looked up the Enneagram and took the assessment to see where I landed. Sure enough, I stood an Eight—the Challenger—just as my friend had shared months earlier. Here is the description of Enneagram Type 8, "The Challenger":

> Eights are self-confident, strong, and assertive. Protective, resourceful, straight-talking, and decisive, but can also be ego-centric and domineering. Eights feel they must control their environment, especially people, sometimes becoming confrontational and intimidating. Eights typically have problems with their tempers and with allowing themselves to be vulnerable. *At their Best*: self-mastering, they use their strength to improve others' lives, becoming heroic, magnanimous, and inspiring.

> • Basic Fear: Of being harmed or controlled by others

> • Basic Desire: To protect themselves (to be in control of their own life and destiny) ...

> • Key Motivations: Want to be self-reliant, to prove their strength and resist weakness, to be important in their world, to dominate the environment, and to stay in control of their situation.[21]

As I read about the Challenger, I understood myself better; many descriptions fit, and I saw myself differently. As I read about the strengths and weaknesses, it wrapped up my life with a pretty bow on top. I remained motionless, drawn inward while soul-searching, trying to make sense of how this new understanding would shape my path toward healing. The lifelong struggle I carried centered around control and vulnerability, and my refusal to show weakness rose unmistakably to the surface as I read my personality type. That awareness marked the moment I finally saw how what we cling to for safety can often keep us stuck. Have you ever recognized how tightly you have held onto control—only to discover how deeply it has cost you? That realization became a turning point I could no longer ignore. My strength had been my cage.

Eliminating my root of control was just as hard as dealing with my root of anger. Childhood trauma trained my brain for survival, a conditioning that has taken real effort to unlearn. For me to fully be who I am in Christ, God knew He and I had to pull out all the roots. Pulling roots out of our hearts is rather painful; it's a process, and it takes time. We have to be willing to surrender the deepest hurts of our hearts, to constantly learn to be gentle with ourselves, not clothe ourselves in shame, and to fully trust and rely on God for restoration and healing. Proverbs 3:5–6 (NLT) was a great reminder for me.

Trust in the Lord with all your heart; do not depend on your own understanding. Seek his will in all you do, and he will show you which path to take.

I highly recommend setting aside time daily for God. I'm not talking about a quick five minutes to check off the "I spent time with God" box as you run out the door. I'm talking about whole undivided attention—just you and God—so His Word can penetrate deep into your heart and soul. When you're alone with God, He will reveal things to you that are crucial for your spiritual development. When I finally surrendered every part of myself in obedience, God met me there and began the work of true transformation.

As I followed my root of control beneath the surface, God gently showed me that it had grown as a defense—coiling tightly around a wound I was too afraid to name. Beneath it lived the abandoned places of my heart, places He had never left, and which He patiently waited to heal.

Please scan the QR code to explore the songs that carried my heart when words fell short.

PART TWO: RESET

True rest comes through surrender. When you place your burdens in God's hands, He truly does the rest.

—Constance André

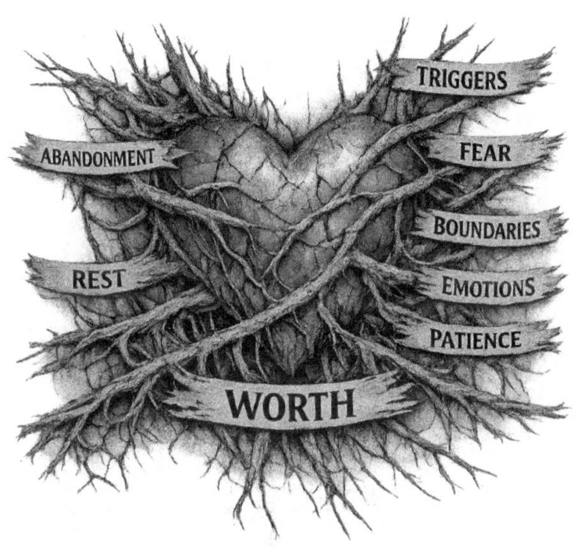

Chapter Five

ABANDONMENT

She stood in the storm, and when the wind did not blow her way,
she adjusted her sails.

—Elizabeth Edwards

During the fall of 2023, I searched for anything that would alleviate my ongoing suffering. I stumbled upon a live blood analysis clinic and figured I should try to see if my blood held any answers as to why I still suffered from pain. I was curious if, under the microscope, my blood would reveal the answers. During the live blood analysis, the technician took a tiny bit of blood from my finger three times, and then we looked at my blood under a microscope. The process looked specifically at my red blood cells, immune system, and the plasma around my cells, all of which I viewed on a big screen.

Although I had not shared a single thing about myself, the technician could tell I had been in accidents. Kind of bizarre, but she knew specifically where in my back and body I had the most trauma and suffered from chronic pain. How blood from my finger could show her this information left me perplexed.

As we looked at the screen in-depth, she pointed out the areas of my body and how she could see the trauma. Clusters of cells stacked on top of one another appeared, and the colour would change around them, indicating trauma. During this analysis, I saw that my liver was working overtime and that several of my red blood cells were damaged and leaking. This information explained why my blood didn't show the B12 deficiency but taking the B12 vitamin fixed the way I felt. When I asked why my red blood cells were leaking, she shared that stress was likely the culprit. The truth hit me hard: my liver was in drastic need of help. Years of chronic stress had damage it, and I could no longer ignore what my body was revealing.

I left the appointment with supplements and an intense six-week eating plan to assist my body in recovery, especially my liver. I had heard several opinions that food could be a contributing factor to the pain I experienced, so this was no surprise. The plan eliminated nearly everything in the food chain. The list of what I could consume became quite small and was based around protein. The eating plan turned out to be a true challenge as it eliminated caffeine as well. However, even with eating this way and changing what I could about my lifestyle for six weeks, I did not notice any positive change in my pain levels. Disappointed that the nerve pain persisted and I still could not walk well, this solidified for me that the foods I ate were not the root cause.

Shortly after this adventure, one of my colleagues referred me to a physiotherapist who specialises in Integrated Systems Model treatments. This service is a specialized assessment model focused on finding the primary region of the body that, when corrected, improves a person's function and performance. I patiently waited for the appointment, and near the end of October, the day finally arrived. Hope filled my being, and my gut confirmed this might be the answer to fixing my pain. Perhaps the physiotherapist would have a different perspective on what we were possibly missing.

At the physiotherapist appointment, I explained in substantial detail everything my body had gone through up to that point. All the therapists I'd seen (counsellors, massage therapist, physiotherapist, chiropractor) agreed my body had been put through the wringer, and they often referred to me as "the perfect storm." I was a jigsaw puzzle, and they were working together to try to solve it.

As the physiotherapist assessed me, he shared that my whole skeletal system seemed twisted, even the bones in my face. Although this wasn't a great diagnosis, I had hope that we were getting to the root of the problem. He shared that my pelvis was extremely rotated, as well as my ribs. Actually, four different sections in my ribs were rotated, causing the muscles, ligaments, and tendons along my spine to be twisted up, similar to a rope.

Over the coming months, he focused on stabilizing my pelvis and ribs. The first day he treated me, fear crept in as IMS needling was applied to my neck and back to release stubborn tension. Remember I had experienced IMS once before, shortly after my second accident, and it had caused a severe setback. That history left me understandably wary. Eight spots in my neck were extremely painful as the needles went in.

Two in particular brought me to tears and took my breath away. Just as with my first IMS treatment six months earlier, my body felt extremely sore for the next week. In spite of the first week's soreness, I continued to see this physiotherapist every week in the hope that my body would soon be fixed.

My pelvis and ribs—the structural part of my body—started to settle, unfortunately, my muscles would flare up and spasm in my back. The process of unwinding my skeletal system took months; however, after four months, I could see we were making progress. The terrible weeks seemed to dominate, which apparently goes along with the healing journey. One step forward, three steps back.

It seemed that whenever I made progress in my physical healing, God would knock at my heart's door again. Without question, the Holy Spirit called me to dig out the root of abandonment. I believe what stirred the root of abandonment was a disagreement I had with my closest friend. We simply could not see eye to eye on a significant matter, and both of us had hurt feelings because of our opinions. So she decided to take a break from our friendship. Neither of us knew for how long, but we both knew we had our own issues to work on, and a timeout was best. As the saying goes, "absence makes the heart grow fonder."

What blindsided me the most during this phase of my journey were the feelings that surfaced. The truth is, friends have been an essential part of my life, more than family, if I'm honest; and they were my safe haven growing up. The fact that my closest friend, the one who knew me best, appeared to be abandoning me left a huge gaping hole—a hole I initially didn't think I would recover from.

Over the next month, I went through all the emotions linked with abandonment: emotions of anger, rejection, sadness, ingrained hurt, betrayal, feeling disrespected, and loneliness, but eventually, I came to acceptance. As I thought back on my life's journey, I could see the gamut of emotions as a pattern. I had been clinging to deep hurt and pain left behind by those who walked out on me. Friends that disappeared when I needed them most, childhood wounds of abandonment that didn't heal, and a husband consumed by his work. All of it pointed to one painful truth: abandonment had become a much deeper root than I was willing to admit.

I am a firm believer that everything happens for a reason, so I knew the trials I faced at that time played a part in my healing journey—another stepping stone, if you will. In my heart, I also knew God intended me to be at this place of healing; He had a plan. The feelings I experienced were for a reason. By this point, God had shown me the process; I just had to dive in and be willing to open yet another closed-off area of my heart. Trusting His plan while enduring emotional and physical suffering is a struggle; however, we need to trust His process and timeline, not our own. This is something I am still learning to accept, and at times I struggle with it.

It took me a few weeks to wrap my mind around the hurt that surfaced with this root of abandonment. It devastated me to have another layer stacked on top of the existing traumatic layers.

A few weeks later, I flew to Puerto Vallarta, Mexico—my happy place, for a week of soul-searching and self-reflection. Some thought I was running away from my problems; how could I escape the pain I felt entangled in when it ran away with me? I just wanted to feel healthy. I wanted to be happy and experience joy instead of all the misery and heartache. I knew long hours sitting on the beach, sun on my skin, eyes fixed on the endless ocean, was exactly where I needed to be to finally surrender the deepest parts of my hurt. I don't know what it is, but whenever I'm on a beach staring into the ocean, it's as if I'm in God's presence, and He is sitting right beside me.

I understood that the real work toward healing had to continue internally. The issues surfacing required my full attention, which meant being alone, free from distractions, so I could focus on God and the healing process—especially after everything I had experienced and overcome in recent years.

With the endless ocean before me, I started reading a book called *Waymaker: Finding the Way to the Life You've Always Dreamed Of*.[22] Certain comments spoke to me through the author's journey. One phrase that grabbed my immediate attention was: "to know someone is to stand a thousand times over the grave of who they once were, and then walk with them on the way to further knowing the inner terrain of who they are becoming."[23] Deep, isn't it? I longed for exactly that, for those closest to me to walk with me through this turbulent season, to forget who I had been, and to embrace the positive changes I made. Another truth echoed loudly within me: "When you're lost in a mess of difficulty, you find you're found when you simply know your identity, *beloved*."[24] As I pondered that quote, I concluded that *I* did not really know *my* true identity.

While sitting under the cabana, staring out at God's beautiful creation, tears welled up. God started stirring my soul, and the lyrics of a song broke into my reverie. While listening to "Hold On" by Brandon Ray featuring Lauren Weintraub, I heard,

I've been where you are, you know the part where things
are hopeless, Searchin' through the dark and find your
heart in all the broken . . . Hold on, when you wanna let
go.[25]

So many thoughts were racing through my mind as I tried to process everything that had happened up to that point. All the signs, phrases, people, situations . . . how things would simply line up, and especially what God had revealed to me at just the right moments. It had been a stunning process, to say the least. The more I reflected, tears of devastation, hurt, sadness, frustration, rejection, and betrayal flowed. Each stung as it mixed with the salty air. I focused on praying to try to release the cemented emotions I harboured, and I could visualise them entering the ocean and being swept away. God felt so close and washed me with peace. I made huge progress with emotional healing on that beach. But there was another setback rounding the corner.

As I attempted my muscle-strengthening exercises the physiotherapist had provided, I sadly injured my left foot and lost the ability to walk. Ironically, my right foot—the one that had caused so much nerve pain—was now healthier from days spent barefoot in the sand. Meanwhile, my left foot swelled and caused agony with every step. I thought being in a tranquil place without the stress of everyday life would support my nervous system so it could relax. Then the curveball. It's almost as if God said to me, "You thought you were going to accomplish what? I have another plan for you." It grieved me deeply to face another setback. Each time I release deep emotional pain, my body seems to answer with fresh physical suffering.

As I headed home, I felt exposed and humiliated being pushed through the airport in a wheelchair. I wrestled with thoughts of how others would perceive me. As irrational as it sounds, that moment revealed a painful truth—I struggled to accept myself and recognize my own worth. A familiar phrase from a dear friend echoed in my heart: *You are seeking validation from outside sources.*

Once I arrived home, I elevated my foot for two weeks and iced it while using my medical device to heal my new injury. This forced me to slow down, so I kept reading, surrendering, and challenging the struggle within. I found myself in the midst of a severe uprooting, caught in a storm of emotions that kept relentlessly surfacing.

However, one day a thought entered my mind—one I believe the Holy Spirit gently gave me. I sensed my friendship with my best friend had been put on hold because I had unknowingly placed her on a pedestal. My entire life, I had looked up to her and strived to be like her: to be a faithful, patient, loving, kind, and compassionate person. In my eyes, she represented the *perfect* Christian. But suddenly, the truth became clear. We are all flawed. Not one of us is better than another. We all have our battles and internal scars we are quietly learning to live with.

At that moment, I remembered a sermon Shawn Johnson had preached about how we appear put together on highlight reels and look blessed on social media or in public when, behind closed doors, we are wounded and falling apart. Then God asked me a question that stopped me cold: *Why can't you be that Christian?* I could hear a pin drop. Deep down, I knew the answer. I was no longer the little girl who needed mentoring. I had grown into a strong, faithful servant, and I had become an equal to my friend. This revelation shook me. Before this, I believed I could not measure up to the standard she had unknowingly set. But God gently affirmed the truth: I am capable. I am worthy. And I deserved to take my rightful place—equal to anyone else. I didn't realize it then, but this revelation was part of a much larger process—one that would soon be deeply connected to my worth.

Some of the memories I had to process regarding this root of abandonment were from childhood. A few in particular were of me standing on the driveway crying, begging my father to take me as he drove off with my brothers in the truck. All of a sudden, several memories like this surfaced. This is where the root of abandonment started. These feelings scarred me deeply as a young child. I could not comprehend why he left me behind, what I had done wrong, or why I was not enough to be chosen.

Another memory demanded processing: my father's sudden death in my early twenties. During that tragic week, my husband had immersed himself in work, making him less accessible to me in my time of need. His actions drove a severe wedge between us, as I could not understand why he placed work before me. Then the questions came again. "What did I ever do to deserve this response? Why does he not love me? Why am I not important enough for him to be with me?"

So often, people don't know how to respond, so they just bury their heads in the sand or run away. I've been one of those individuals, and I will confess it is easier to sweep things under the rug than to face hardship. Dave's actions that week cut me deeply. I didn't understand how he could say he loved me when he literally abandoned me in the toughest hours of my life. Now, as God clearly worked through my root of abandonment, I acknowledged that I'd never forgiven Dave for his actions. I'd buried the scars deep inside, but they were reflected in my responses to him over the coming years. The time had come to lay down this deep hurt and trust that God would heal my heart and pain.

As I continued to process painful memories, the events that took place no longer held any power over me. For this to move forward, I had to surrender to God the pain and emotions bound to abandonment. I could not hold anything back. He was the only one who could heal my fractured heart and the deep pain with which I lived. Unfortunately, I had borne these scars most of my life. These wounds helped shape the person I became and how I responded when triggered by feelings of abandonment.

Pressing on, it became clear I had to discover my true identity. God is the only source of comfort and healing capable of providing the relief we need. When I accepted that I am a child of God, made in His image, my perspective shifted—and with that came the truth that I am enough, and I am loved. By surrendering control and trusting God, what pain, trauma, and fear once made impossible became possible. I could finally see myself as God sees me: His precious child. As the lens through which I viewed life began to change, peace once again returned. God had spoken hope into my pain—but I was not finished yet; roots still remained.

Please scan the QR code to listen to the songs that soothed my heart during the healing of my root of abandonment.

Chapter Six

REST

Rest is not a matter of doing absolutely nothing. Rest is repair.

—Daniel W. Josselyn

As February 2024 rolled in, excitement filled the air as we travelled to a TobyMac concert in Abbotsford. Years prior, I had missed his concert due to unforeseen circumstances, so this was my second chance. My daughter and I drove down with friends of ours, and I figured I could try riding in the back seat and see how it went. Up until that point, I'd been anxious about riding in a vehicle as the driver or passenger, and the nerve pain sure made its presence known regardless of where I rode.

By the day of the concert, I was barely holding it together. Nerve pain consumed the left side of my body while the right foot pulsed relentlessly. I could not walk without pain. I could not sit comfortably. I shifted my suffering—standing for a few minutes at a time, then sitting, then standing again—caught in a loop my body refused to release me from.

As we waited for the concert to begin, emotions weighed heavily on me—pain layered with deep frustration. While the opening act sang, I wept as the lyrics pierced my soul. I fought what was rising inside me, struggling to yield to the grief and exhaustion I carried. All the artists' songs broke me. This was the first concert I ever attended where I wept almost the entire time. My daughter and friends looked over at me from time to time, not knowing how to support me, but they could see the weight of the battle I carried.

I vividly remember the intermission. As I attempted to climb the stairs, an overwhelming heaviness rushed me—as though I were dragging a boulder behind me, barely able to lift my legs. I had not experienced this kind of heaviness before, yet deep down I sensed things were coming to a head. I didn't know if I could sit through the rest of the concert or even function. The pain seared, and the pharmaceutical medications did not touch it. With that crushing heaviness layered on top of all the emotions rising to the surface, I was unravelling.

When I finally crept back to my seat and TobyMac took the stage, he opened with "Help Is on the Way." The lyrics pierced my heart.

> I heard your heart, I see your pain
> Out in the dark, out in the rain
> Feel so alone, feel so afraid
> I heard you pray in Jesus' name . . .
> Help is on the way.[26]

Instantly, I wept. My heart was unbearably heavy, and in that sacred moment, I knew God spoke directly to me. Using the lyrics of TobyMac's song, God reminded me that I was not alone and that help truly was on the way.

The next day, as we headed home, I slipped my earbuds in and listened to Christian music the entire drive. I stared out the window as we passed through God's breathtaking creation, tears streaming as the lyrics sank deep in my soul. I poured out the cries of my heart in prayer, fixing my gaze on the mountains and imagining God there—hearing every word, sensing the depth of my hurt—as I begged and pleaded for relief. My friends likely did not know what I carried or how to help, but they knew enough to see I was not in a good place.

As I tried to process everything that had occurred, my mind replayed the moment I walked up the stairs, how weighed down I felt, and the fact that "Help Is on the Way" was the first song TobyMac sang. My curiosity stirred, and I knew those lyrics were a message meant for me. I believed better days were coming, yet in the midst of the relentless emotional and physical pain, I could no longer see a way out. At an all-time low, I felt utterly hopeless—hurting in every imaginable way. It took everything I had to make it home in one piece. When I did, I had Dave meet me in town with my swim gear so I could go straight to the pool and initiate my physiotherapy stretches.

As I stepped into the pool and began my stretches, tears mixed with the water as pain surged through every movement. I pleaded silently for relief. I would not wish nerve pain on my worst enemy. It is a relentless torment, the type of pain that could drive someone to do something they would never imagine when they were well. With little relief from the pool or the pleading, I gathered myself and decided to take time off.

The month of February remained challenging as my physical limitations forced me to rest. Rest is not an effortless thing for me; I may sit and rest for an hour or two, but to sit and rest for weeks? I took six weeks off during this time, working little, trying to focus on recuperating my emotional and physical health. While sitting on my couch reading, I suddenly had a vision of Jesus reaching out his hand to me while He walked on water, and Matthew 11:28b (NLT) came to my mind.

"Come to me, all of you who are weary and carry heavy burdens, and I will give you rest."

It is extremely hard to put ourselves first and not have a task list running through our minds. The constant struggle between our mind and our body is intense, and it certainly wore me down. If it had not been for my faith during this time, I do not know how I would have survived. God provided the strength to face another day, just as the Bible states in Philippians 4:13 (NLT): "For I can do everything through Christ, who gives me strength." I kept reminding myself to put one foot in front of the other, one day at a time; I could not think of the future. I had to live in the moment, truly in the moment. I had never slowed down to this pace before, but obviously, my body needed a reprieve.

At my next physiotherapy appointment, I could no longer ignore what my body was telling me. IMS needling felt like it was reactivating trauma, so I asked that we stop to pursue an alternative approach to calming my nervous system. The flare-ups were constant, and I could not get ahead with the constant triggers. Healing simply felt out of reach. With no clear guidance from my doctor, the physiotherapist trusted my instinct and redirected our sessions toward calming my nervous system. My muscles simply would not respond while my nervous system vibrated on high. I thought to myself, *What do I have to lose?* I decided to give it a few months and see if this shift would bring relief.

The insurance companies finally approved counselling, and by mid-February, I began attending weekly sessions. The timing felt intentional, as if my body was finally ready to face what my mind had been avoiding. During those visits, the counsellor helped me process the layers of emotions, trauma, and triggers that the accidents had caused or brought forth. We used all sorts of different methods, but one that stands out is Emotional Freedom Technique (EFT) Tapping.

Not long after my weekly sessions began, the name of a certain individual came to mind. I knew the Holy Spirit had laid her name on my heart, but I did not know why. As I searched for her online, I discovered that she had written a book on emotional and physical healing through Christ-centered emotional freedom techniques. If that is not a sign, especially in the middle of what I was enduring, I don't know what is. I knew I needed to read her book and trusted that God would reveal answers through the pages. Without hesitation, I ordered it and waited patiently for its arrival.

Following one of my most intense counselling sessions, I wrote the letter included here without any sense of what it would stir or reveal. I simply sat down and started writing. Then it appeared that my hand had a mind of its own, and the words poured out onto the paper. When I finished and read the letter to myself, I wept uncontrollably. This letter has become an essential part of my healing, offering exactly what I needed during this phase of my journey.

October 2024

Dear Constance,

First off, I want to let you know you are worthy of My love. You are valued and loved more than anything. I see your heart and know your deep pain, and I release you of all the guilt, shame, and regret you may have. I know you have been working so hard at following My footsteps, guidance, and words. I am with you all the time and release the pain and hurt. You are so precious to Me—a light and a beacon. I chose you because you are capable of more than you know. My power will help see you through and guide your steps. You are exactly where you need to be; have mercy on yourself. Be kind, compassionate, and loving to all, including those who have hurt you. Let your actions speak, be quick to listen, and seek Me in prayer always. Come to Me when you're hurting, lonely, and sad. You will find rest and peace in My presence. You are My child and absolutely worthy. Don't doubt the process and timeline; I have set things in motion. Be gentle on yourself and rest. Rest your weary soul and heart. I promise, I will never leave you nor forsake you. Perseverance produces character and wisdom. I have plans and a purpose for you, My precious girl, just trust and obey My timing. Keep with the plans I have for you, endure, but never lose hope and faith. I love you, dear child. Now go in peace.

Jesus

While the Holy Spirit wrote this letter to me, I believe He wrote it through me to help you as well. Take just a moment to go back and reread it, addressing it to yourself this time.

In rest, God quieted the striving and silenced the voices that had long measured my value. In that stillness, He began to reveal a deeper truth—that our worth has never been something to earn but something He already declared.

Please scan the QR code to hear the songs that guided me as music became the bridge between my pain and His presence.

PART THREE: RESTORE

—Constance André

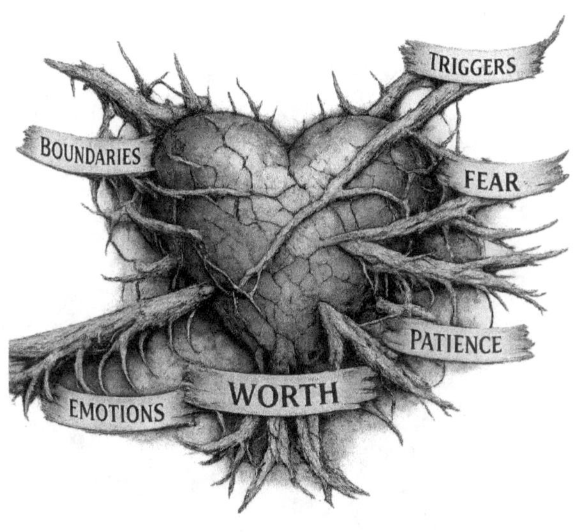

Chapter Seven
WORTH

*Owning our story and loving ourselves through that process
is the bravest thing that we'll ever do.*

—Brené Brown

I dare to ask the question, *Do you truly feel worthy?* My answer surfaced quietly; for most of my life, I wavered about my worth. An odd realization, especially since I am a perfectionist who worked tirelessly to prove my worth through what I could bring to the table. I had not seen the correlation between not knowing who I truly was and my sense of worth. That is, until God began moving in that area of my life. Then I came across an eye-opening quote that slapped me: "You can't hide from yourself and heal at the same time."[27]

Digging out the root of worth all started with earning an incentive trip to a "Fast Start" manager retreat in Scottsdale, Arizona, with the medical device business I'd started. This moment would mark the beginning of uncovering yet another buried root.

For as long as I can remember, I refused to set goals, believing that if I never reached for them, I could never fail—or let anyone down. After falling in love with my medical device and the company behind it, I set a goal to qualify for a trip overseas so I could be amongst global distributors. But I did not even allow myself to imagine earning the trip—it felt impossible. After all, for a small-town girl from Manitoba, I had learned to believe opportunities like this were not meant for someone like me.

As the weeks went on, I carried on with my daily life, working as best as I could while limited by the nerve pain. As the time came near, I could see that I had a remarkably good chance of meeting this goal and allowed myself to believe that I could for the first time. Well, about a month later, I earned the incentive trip to Mallorca, Spain. I still could not fathom that I had achieved this. I was heading overseas, about to be in the presence of the founder, chief executive officer, global doctors, and management. I remained in disbelief. I had not had the privilege to travel overseas before, so this seemed monumental. Even more surreal, I had been with this company for only nine months, yet I had earned my place alongside individuals who had worked in the business for years—even decades. This trip was a dream come true and meant far more to me than I ever could have imagined.

Shortly after earning my incentive trip, I received a call from the corporate office—the one that would change everything. The director of sales asked me to speak at the North American distributor kickoff in

January. They wanted to recognize my achievements and asked me to share insights regarding how I'd accomplished what I had in such a short time. I was speechless. No one had ever recognized my abilities like this before, and now they were asking this small-town girl to influence the lives of a thousand people through my story. It felt unreal.

Honored and on cloud nine, I knew instantly I would be sharing that faith was my driving source. All the lessons I had learned up to this point were a result of my faith and willingness to listen and respond in obedience to God. I also knew that when I took a stand and declared my faith publicly, the spiritual enemy would start attacking me. Still, nothing could have prepared me for what came next.

As my flights drew closer, anticipation built for the journey ahead—to Scottsdale, Arizona, and Mallorca, Spain. A quiet certainty settled in me that these trips carried purpose. More than once, others had spoken of something in my voice—a presence, an ability to draw people in without force. Still, I had not yet recognized that God moved through my voice, especially through public speaking, touching lives in ways I could not see. I believed God had planned this trip to Spain so that I might have another story to share—but I was unaware of how much God still intended to reveal to me.

As if my story didn't have enough setbacks, to my dismay, another one struck, one I had not anticipated.

On May 1, 2024, while driving to my doctor's office on a four-lane stretch of highway, I heard the crunch of metal as I passed a line of vehicles. I glanced in my rearview mirror and saw a bright blue pickup truck halfway in my lane. Instantly, I knew—he had hit me. A headache surged as I frantically pulled my Jeep over before the stoplight. Moments later, my body began to shake, and my thoughts scattered. My brain felt like mush; I could not connect the dots or think clearly. When I stepped out of my vehicle to speak to the man who had hit me, anger took over. "You didn't look! How did you not see me?!" I yelled. "What were you thinking? You do not know what this is going to do to me." The older gentleman apologized repeatedly, but I told him he didn't understand. I explained that I was currently recovering from injuries from previous accidents—and now this. I feared the physical outcome more than anything. The pain. The setback. And this occurred a month and a half before my Spain trip. As I walked to the passenger side of my Jeep, the damage came fully into view. He had scraped and torn the entire side; my door pulled outward and kinked, and a deep gouge ran front to back. He'd sideswiped the length of my vehicle. After we exchanged information, I slid back inside my mangled Jeep and wept. Disbelief washed over me—another accident. Shock settled in, leaving me numb.

I phoned Dave to inform him of what had occurred, and his response astounded me. He focused on the damage to the vehicle, and not once did he ask if I was okay. He didn't offer to come get me, to assist with picking up our daughter . . . nothing. Instead, I found myself defending my words and actions. This was not my fault.

My daughter was about ten blocks away at an appointment, so I began driving in her direction. I only made it four blocks from the accident scene and had to pull over. My breathing became shallow, and a panic attack took hold. I immediately phoned my sister-in-law, and she calmly talked me through it until I could breathe again. I know without a doubt that she was praying for me as well.

After picking Raelyn up, shock consumed me as I struggled to drive home. In retrospect, I see how I should not have been driving with the mental impairment that comes with shock. Distraught after the day's events, I reached out to a few friends once we arrived home and asked for prayer. One of them pleaded with me to see a doctor and document this new accident and the injuries. She assured me that it would impact my existing injuries and claims and needed to be documented.

Later that afternoon, as I tried to gather myself on my deck for about an hour, I stared into the field in disbelief. I could not wrap my head around why this had happened again. *Why me? What did I do to deserve this?* The more time passed, the more I could feel my back seizing, layer by layer, and the all-too-familiar pain returning. Mentally, I felt doomed, with nothing positive left to grasp.

I decided to take my friend's advice and made my way to the walk-in clinic to get looked at. Dave was nowhere to be found, so I drove myself in his vehicle and arranged for a friend to meet me at the clinic. The doctor confirmed that all the signs I showed were symptoms of PTSD. He proceeded to hand me a refill of anti-inflammatories and painkillers along with instructions to lie low, rest, and stay out of a vehicle. *No problem*, I thought, by no means will I step close to that Jeep.

When I got home, I wrapped my head with my medical device to calm my nervous system. It did not help with my mental state, though, and a deep, heavy cloud consumed me. I felt hopeless, and in all honesty, I just wanted to die. I remember telling my husband I didn't want to live anymore. I was tired of being robbed of my life and enduring constant pain. I could not understand why God had allowed me to go through another accident and why I had to suffer now with PTSD on top of everything else. I truly felt at my breaking point, stripped of purpose, and completely beaten down. For days, I did not want to get out of bed. I would not get dressed; I just lay there crying into my pillow. I asked Dave several times to stay with me as I wept, and yet, once again, he chose the ranch work over me.

I have heard in conversation several times before that people cannot understand how and why a faithful Christian would end their life. Frankly, you will not understand mental illness and the impact it has on a person's mind unless you experience it yourself. I have witnessed family and friends suffer through mental illness, and I will say that I never, in my darkest nightmares, would have thought I would go through it. When everything seems heavy and you perceive hopelessness, combined with relentless pain, it is quite simple to think *the* thoughts.

I am a very faithful person; I continuously strive to implement what God has asked of me, and yet I remained crippled with such dark thoughts during this season of my life. I believed the lies that ran through my mind during the darkest hours I endured. *I am all alone; no one cares about me; I am not worthy of healing; I have no friends and worst of all, the lie that my family is better off without me.*

When darkness speaks to you, which lies feel hardest to silence—and what might it look like for you to gently question them? Can we pause long enough to ask whether they sound like the voice of God—or the voice of pain?

A wise mentor reminded me that my life had borne fruit and that Satan wanted to stop me; the spiritual battle is real, just as Ephesians 6:10–12 (NLT) states:

> *A final word: Be strong in the Lord and in his mighty power. Put on all of God's armor so that you will be able to*

stand firm against all strategies of the devil. For we are not fighting against flesh-and-blood enemies, but against evil rulers and authorities of the unseen world, against mighty powers in this dark world, and against evil spirits in the heavenly places.

After I heard my mentor's wisdom and read the above scripture, I knew Satan had me where he wanted me, crippled. I mean, I could not impact anyone's life for God while experiencing this kind of mental state, hardly functioning myself.

The third accident took place on a Wednesday, and by Saturday morning, I could sense the darkness lift. It was similar to how dew lifts in the morning as the sun rises. I could sense hope being restored and knew God would get me through this setback. The question remained: would I be able to make my upcoming trips to Scottsdale, Arizona, and Mallorca, Spain? I still could not comprehend why God allowed me to enter this place again—a third accident, additional layers of pain you could not have prepared me for.

Then, in His perfect timing, God opened the door and showed me the reason behind it all. While at the medical clinic for a full spinal X-ray, I left my appointment twenty minutes early and walked down the hall. I came across an elderly lady who struggled to walk, crippled by pain. I watched individuals almost bump into her, and no one offered to assist. I could not believe my eyes and thought, *What kind of world do I live in to see such selfish behavior?* I offered her a hand and helped her to a chair so she could sit down while waiting for her ride. After sitting with her for a few moments, I knew why we had met and that I needed to share my medical device with her to support her health. God wove my injuries into His purpose, placing me in the path of someone who needed what I had to offer.

Over the next month, she used the medical device, and her ailments became more manageable; she was very pleased. I could see physical changes in her. She stood upright and walked without her cane. A distance that would have taken her five minutes to walk now took sixty seconds; it was mind-blowing. I cannot count the times she has told me I am her guardian angel and that I saved her life, that if it wasn't for me, she would no longer be here. At one time she had contemplated ending her life. God placed me in her path, at just the right moment, as a lifeline to lift her out of the dark pit she was enduring. God used me to speak life into her and gently lead her back to Him. Even today, I often pray for her and take her out for coffee so she is not alone. Every time we are together, she is so grateful and has a big smile on her face. Witnessing what I went through and how God used my pain for His glory made the third accident worthwhile, even though the worst of it was yet to come. When joy fills your heart as you lift someone else up, there is no greater feeling in the world.

About three weeks after this third impact, I had a warming and tingling sensation in my right inner shin. The sensation lasted about thirty seconds, and I was certain it was nerve-related. For a few days, I encountered this unusual sensation and then, all of a sudden, the nerve pain in my right foot vanished! I could walk! After sixteen months of not being able to walk freely, I simply cannot tell you how exciting it felt to be able to walk without intense pain. I will never take the simple act of walking for granted. Each day, I thank God for the gift of healing He has given me.

As I continued with my healing and hydrotherapy at the pool, my focus turned to strengthening my leg muscles, which had not functioned well for such a long time. I needed to get the muscles in my right leg working properly again. When I tried to walk short distances, it seemed the muscles in my calves and legs were struggling, causing a huge amount of discomfort and pain. Despite no longer having the nerve pain in my right foot, my muscles had to reestablish their proper responses and positioning, and in doing this, I still endured immense pain. I mean, I get it, they hadn't done their job properly in sixteen months. How would my muscles remember to work again? Up against the clock, thoughts of being able to walk for Spain plagued me, so I gave it my all for the next month.

A dear friend and business coach I met inspired me to read the book *Worthy: How to Believe You Are Enough and Transform Your Life* by Jamie Kern Lima.[28] She encouraged me that *Worthy* would be a real game changer for me. An eye-opener! Well, she truly was not kidding.

At the end of May, I flew to Scottsdale for the Fast Start manager retreat. As soon as I settled into my seat on the plane, I started reading the book *Worthy*. From the moment I opened it, certain phrases immediately caught my attention. "For the 80 percent of women who don't believe they're enough. . . . 91 percent of girls and women who don't love their bodies. . . . When you believe you're fundamentally not enough and unworthy as a person, it's a lie. The time to unlearn that lie has come."[29]

While I continued reading, the words stopped me once again. Jamie powerfully states, "Self-doubt, unworthiness, and fear cause us to dim our soul's light. . . . The moment you learn to believe that you are worthy, your entire life, the past and future generations of your family, and your entire world change for the better."[30] I immediately knew God brought this book into my path for a specific reason. He called me to restore my worth.

As I continued reading, I concluded that we do not rise to the level of our dreams. Instead, we remain limited by what we believe we are worthy of. Our lives tend to reflect not what we desire but what we believe we deserve. We live at the level of our self-worth. Many phrases sank deep into the core of my soul. I could see that I didn't value myself or see my worth. My heart sank as it dawned on me that I did not feel loved.

At that moment, I faced a huge dilemma and understood that if I wanted to experience peace, I had to change how I felt. I wanted to feel worthy, I really did, but I didn't know how or where to start. Then I came across a quote that stopped me in my tracks: "Are you not letting new people love you because of how old people have hurt you?" Those words became my path—the door God used to open and point me toward where healing needed to begin.

While I read chapter one, self-worth and self-confidence stood out to me. I realized that life can rearrange itself around you, but real change only happens when something shifts within. For years, I have tried to live by the mantra, "Be the change you wish to see in the world," but after reading those specific words, I perceived, through all my attempts, that I truly did not change on the inside. I was not willing to open the deepest parts of pain that were buried within my heart and soul. And therein lay my problem.

Self-worth is an inner knowing—rooted deep within—that you are enough and worthy of love and belonging exactly as you are. Self-confidence is how you measure yourself: your belief in your ability to rise to challenges, try new things, and succeed. Unlike self-worth, confidence is often shaped by external circumstances and can easily waver.

Then the author, Jamie, shared something that instantly clicked. "Self-worth is your foundation. Self-confidence is the house you build on top of it. Your house will only ever be as secure as the foundation it's built upon."[31]

Intrigued, I became motivated to learn more about self-worth. I needed to figure out how to reclaim mine. I understood that confidence alone can still leave us fearful—afraid of rejection, failure, and the unknown. But when self-worth is strong, it anchors a resilient core that cannot be easily diminished. From that foundation, you rise with unwavering strength into all you were born to become. I felt as if Jamie was going straight for my jugular, not holding anything back but laying it all on the line. I wept as I continued reading.

It seemed I was completely fragmented in an area I had not realized until this point—a humbling moment for someone who has a lot of confidence. I soon grasped that having self-confidence is equivalent to feeling successful externally while failing internally. That phrase pretty much summed up my entire identity. I worked tirelessly to prove my worth through achievements and a polished facade while inwardly unraveling, in desperate need of healing.

I continued reading, and a powerful phrase sank deep. "As with all newly charted paths, it's almost never a straight line. It is filled with bumps and zigzags and setbacks and detours and wrong turns. . . . The secret to getting what you want is to truly learn to believe you're worthy of it."[32] God knew what I needed, and slowly, one step at a time, He uprooted my entire life. God's timing is perfect, just as Jesus says in John 16:12–13 (NLT),

> *There is so much more I [Jesus] want to tell you [Christ followers], but you can't bear it now. When the Spirit of truth comes [Holy Spirit], he will guide you into all truth. He will not speak on his own but will tell you what he has heard. He will tell you about the future.*

As I continued searching, the phrase "limiting beliefs" repeatedly appeared. So I decided to take a closer look at mine. Limiting beliefs are self-defeating thoughts and assumptions that quietly narrow what we believe is possible for our lives. They can prevent us from achieving our goals and are often deeply ingrained. These beliefs can stem from past experiences, criticism, self-protection patterns, and unconscious conditioning. Internal narratives frequently surface as negative self-talk, subtly discouraging us from taking risks or stepping into new opportunities. Over time, they can fuel procrastination, avoidance, self-doubt, and diminished motivation. Learning to recognize and confront these *false* beliefs becomes a powerful first step toward meaningful personal growth and lasting change.

As I continued working on my mindset, the concept of limiting beliefs began to make sense. I became more aware of my negative internal narrative and started intentionally replacing it with empowering words. I realized those limiting beliefs were deeply intertwined with my self-confidence and sense of self-worth. What negative narratives have you been living by? What might change if you replaced them with more empowering truths?

As part of processing the unworthiness that I carried, I followed Jamie's guidance. I learned that facing rejection required me to confront the quiet definitions I had been assigning to it—meanings that told me failure diminished my worth or that being rejected confirmed I was not enough. When rejection or failure appears, the first place it often lands is in our sense of worth. Without realizing it, we assign meaning to those moments, telling ourselves what they say about who we are and what we are capable of. Yet those definitions are rarely chosen with intention; they form automatically, quietly shaping our identity and limiting our willingness to try.

As my understanding of worth deepened, I chose to redefine rejection. I started to see it not as evidence of inadequacy but as an invitation to grow, stretch, and trust God more fully. This shift allowed me to revisit moments from my past that had once wounded me deeply and assign them new meaning rooted in resilience rather than shame. Healing begins when we challenge those narratives and replace them with truths that affirm our worth rather than diminish it. Over time, rejection ceased to threaten my sense of worth. It lost its power to define me because my value was no longer tied to outcomes or approval but anchored in who God says I am. How might your life shift if the moments you once labeled as rejection were instead invitations to trust God more deeply and see your worth through His eyes?

I experienced firsthand the strength my mindset held over me during this phase of my healing. I noticed when I would glance at myself in the mirror that I usually put myself down. Comments such as "I'm not pretty enough" and "I'm too heavy" would affirm I did not look the way I thought I should. I had to learn to love and accept myself and change the label I had created for myself. One of the practices I implemented involved looking at myself in the mirror staring at my eyes while saying kind things to myself. Let me be honest—this feels incredibly awkward and deeply emotional in the beginning. As I looked deep into my eyes, it felt as though my soul looked back at me. I saw such heaviness and sadness—as if the weight of the world held me back. It was as though my true, authentic self was trapped and looking for a way out—buried alive.

As I started giving myself empowering labels such as "I am beautiful, I am worthy, I am loved, I am going to recover," and "I am intelligent," I could not control the grief streaming down my face. The emotional release it provided was huge. After all the healing I had been through, I still had no idea I carried such a massive load of pain, grief, and emotion. Looking back, I am astonished I could function at all with everything God revealed. Emotions just kept pouring out of me—every tiny piece removed, repaired, and restored. I was being transformed from the inside out, and though it was a painful experience, it was an utterly freeing one as well. Remember that your worth is not tied to your past. Embrace it, learn from it, then boldly move forward.

I encourage you to look in a mirror and truly see your authentic self through your own eyes. Please look at your soul that lies behind the eyes and tap into it; reaffirm, encourage, strengthen, and build up that soul struggling to survive. When we implement this kind of deep soul care, we free ourselves from bondage. This is a process that requires dedication, love, and grace; it cannot be rushed or completed overnight.

While at the Fast Start manager retreat in Scottsdale, Arizona, I met about fifty people from around North America, including the CEO. We all shared our stories, and it was evident that divine intervention brought us all there. Some amazing people encouraged my entrepreneurial spirit and treated me with such kindness. They pampered me and recognized me for my efforts. It truly felt as though I had won the lottery.

Finally, the day came to head to Barcelona, Spain. I left from the Calgary, Alberta, airport, and for the first time in my life, I snuggled into premium class seating. As the flight attendant had escorted me onto the plane, I stood amazed to see the room I had in the cabin. The comfy seats that reclined were accompanied by spectacular service. Before I settled in, I was offered a mimosa. *Heck yeah*, I figured! I could not believe this was truly happening. I had asked my husband to join me several times, but as usual, the ranch took precedence, so I traveled alone. However, I thoroughly enjoyed my peace and quiet with no responsibilities; this was fabulous!

When I arrived in Barcelona, I discovered the resort was about forty minutes from the airport. It never dawned on me that the PTSD would throw a monkey wrench into my travel plans. Intense PTSD symptoms plagued me while I rode in the back seat of the taxis as they drove through six lanes of traffic, cutting in and out with horns honking. My nerves frayed, my stomach churned, and I prayed to make it there in one piece. Most of the ride, I closed my eyes and prayed for the strength to make it through. I thought to myself, *How on earth am I going to drive my rental car when I get to the city of Palma? I'm in no condition to drive. I can't deal with this traffic.* I didn't know what to do. All my sightseeing adventure plans were in limbo as I tried to navigate this uncharted territory.

After I arrived at the hotel, I decided I would take the hop-on, hop-off double-decker bus to tour the sights of Barcelona. With the nerve injury on the left side of my body that seemed to come and go as it pleased, I was still unable to walk well, so I hesitated to go in and look at a lot of the sights. I just stayed on the bus and watched from my seat, which felt pretty spectacular in itself.

A few days after arriving in Barcelona, I flew to Palma, picked up my rental car, and attempted to navigate a foreign land with a Spanish-speaking GPS. For the life of me, I could not change the car's GPS to English. I was stuck in traffic, having to decide on the fly which way to turn as I could not understand the GPS instructions. I literally just picked a direction and ventured down the road. A short way later, the physical surroundings confirmed I was headed in the right direction. Phew!

While I toured Palma, I went to see one of the most beautiful cathedrals I'd ever set foot in. The pictures I took simply do not do the Catedral de Mallorca justice.[33] The cathedral was breathtaking and its atmosphere sacred. I sat in the pews, praying and giving thanks for this incredible experience as I soaked in the beautiful architectural design. While walking on the cobbled streets around Catedral de Mallorca and meandering amongst the brick buildings, I truly felt as if I'd entered a movie scene. Horses and buggies transported people through the streets. The culture was unlike anything I had ever seen before.

Then, mid-stride, a loud pop cut through the moment—another setback. The muscle in my right calf, the foot that had already betrayed me for sixteen months, felt torn. In a significant amount of pain, I struggled to move. I slowly limped while trying to suck up the excruciating pain. Finally, I made it to my car and proceeded to take some painkillers. I guess I pushed my leg too much while walking through the large airports. My mind was willing and excited, but my body obviously wasn't ready.

Later that afternoon, as I pulled up to the resort for the "founders challenge," I saw Porsches all around the grounds and even in the boardrooms. I discovered Porsche was filming to launch electric versions of different models. To my surprise, this appeared to be a luxurious resort, and I began to feel like royalty. Even though I struggled to walk and dealt with pain, outwardly I tried to make the best of it; internally, I felt frustrated and overwhelmed.

Once I settled into my room, I hopped on my medical device and started crying, pleading with God for relief. *Here I am, in the most beautiful place I have ever seen, hours before our meeting, and I'm struggling once again.* I could not fathom why God brought me this far, literally across the world *and* in my healing, only to endure setbacks and more suffering. Then I came across another relatable quote that provided answers: "Each setback is a divinely orchestrated setup for what you're destined to do next."[34] Needless to say, the first day I grappled to stay positive and truly soak in the gift of this trip while navigating the setback.

The following day, the corporate team took us to a winery where we held our business meeting amidst the picturesque surroundings. The founder, CEO, and operations manager all addressed the group. We were also asked to share a bit about ourselves. A sense of amazement washed over me as I heard that I was among the one percent of distributors worldwide who had earned this incentive. I knew God helped me; there was no doubt about it. I had the opportunity to mingle with highly accomplished entrepreneurs, learning valuable skills and discovering how to fine-tune myself and my business. The lunch and views were spectacular as the sun blazed down on me.

That evening, they took us to a finca, which is a Spanish country escape or ranch. As we arrived, I saw a beautiful archway intertwined with vines and flowers where they offered us refreshments. As we passed through the archway, Spanish music drifted through the air. A live band played around a pool where hors d'oeuvres and champagne were being served as I mingled amongst the crowd. A few hours later, we followed a small pathway, and the scene took my breath away. I paused silently to take it all in. The table was set as though awaiting a royal wedding—every detail intentional, every element exquisite. The decor: flawless. Emotion welled up as I greatly appreciated this opportunity. I felt a deep gratitude to be there, while others seemed to take all the grandeur for granted. To cap off this flawless evening, Spanish dancers entertained us with a live performance. Words can hardly express how I felt in this place of beauty, wealth, and status. Someone needed to pinch me because I could not believe that I was really there, taking part in this spectacular event.

As the evening faded, I had a chance to talk to the CEO, and I must say she is the kindest, sweetest, most down-to-earth person you'll ever meet. In my woundedness, while thanking her for this incredible gift, I could not hold back the tears. She shared that I am worthy and that I needed to work on my self-worth. She said that I belonged there with everyone else and challenged me to dig deep and conquer this dilemma head-on. I heard her words but was unable to fully receive them at the moment. I could not believe that strangers treated me so kindly and included me in these extravagant events. As I drove myself back to the resort that night, I cried often. My heart wrestled to process the emotions stirring within me and to truly receive the gift of this trip. An internal wall kept those healthy emotions at a distance as I continued to wrestle with my worth.

The following morning, while at my hotel, I picked up *Worthy* and began reading again. I was determined to work through this root and find healing before I left Spain. I came across another section that sank deep as I had this epiphany: when our inner world remains unchanged, nothing external can fill the emptiness for long. Many of us spend our lives believing fulfillment will come once we reach a certain point or achieve a specific outcome. Yet true healing begins when we learn to feel enough right where we are, trusting that God meets us exactly as we are. Unlearning false beliefs and learning to trust both God and the wisdom within us becomes one of the most sacred journeys of our lives.

After the corporate event, I headed north to another resort for a week. I had planned to drive around Mallorca and take in all the small towns while sightseeing. I stopped frequently at breathtaking beaches as I continued to work on my self-worth while allowing my body to rest. On days when I could walk more easily, I did some sightseeing and visited the Cuevas del Drach, a beautiful excursion of four caves located in Mallorca.[35] On other days, I took the scenic route and drove around most of the island, checking out different landscapes and architecture. Other days, I simply relaxed by the pool, listening to the ocean while continuing to work on my root of worth. I was determined to pull out the deeply embedded lie of unworthiness so I could continue healing.

While sitting on the beach observing the most beautiful scene on the Mediterranean Sea, I wept uncontrollably as deep emotions were released. God was working in a mighty way, and Jamie's words kept piercing deeply.

> Two partners live inside a relationship with no idea why it feels so disconnected, lonely, or like the other person is hiding something, when in fact they're both hiding from themselves and their own awareness. You can only experience the depth of love, intimacy, and connection with another person as the depth you love and intimately connect with yourself.[36]

Ouch! Now my biggest problem had become evident to me. Before I could connect deeper with others, I had to learn to truly love and accept myself—to believe my value lies in my *own* worth—because nothing around me, not even my marriage or health, would matter if I could not conquer this task.

"If you don't believe you're worthy of loving yourself unconditionally, it's impossible to find, give, receive, or believe you deserve unconditional love from someone else. We cannot give what we do not have."[37] With God's guidance, I will live out this profound truth, moving in the right direction.

Life is shaped not by what happens to us but by the meaning we assign to those happenings. That meaning stirs our emotions, and those emotions shape our experiences. When we intentionally change the meaning we attach to our circumstances—and truly believe it—everything begins to shift. Disappointment gives way to trust. Self-criticism turns into gratitude. Rejection becomes resilience. Our sense of worth grows. When we transform how we view rejection and failure, we don't just change moments—we change the trajectory of our lives. What might God be inviting you to heal within yourself before anything around you can truly change? What would change in your life if you fully believed your value was inherent and not dependent on your relationships, health, or circumstances?

While working on the redefining process, I knew one of the biggest problems I needed to deal with was taking everything personally. I constantly seemed to take things personally, no matter what the situation, and yet I could not understand why. Part of my struggle stemmed from my lack of self-value or self-love, so I took people's responses to heart, turning them into fuel for my own shame. In doing so, I caused myself unnecessary pain. I had to learn to replace disempowering labels with empowering labels. As humans, we try to avoid pain at all costs because it is part of our survival mechanism, thus how we are wired. When I feel inadequate, unworthy, unlovable, or simply not enough, pain enters the picture. Once I learned to mentally link this pain to the true source, I could tackle the root.

The process of reframing can make rejection less painful; instead of looking at situations or events as failure, I put myself in the other person's shoes. For instance, instead of looking at my career and the nos I heard as rejection, I reframed them by saying, "It's not their time yet; just keep doing what I'm doing; one day it'll pay off," and I moved forward without the situation and outcome hanging over me or replaying in my thoughts.

Reading these words that Jamie shares cemented the reframing process in my mind.

> Imagine your Creator saying to you right now: you weren't rejected. I hid your value from them because

they're not assigned to your destiny. . . . Rejection is redirection. It's simply pointing me in the way of something better that's soon to come. Thank you for this rejection/failure because I trust it's happening for me not to me. Thank you for this rejection/failure because I know it's helping me build the resilience, the muscle, and the strength to carry the weight of my future successes when they happen.[38]

The words rang true as God used them to impact my soul. Quite often, I felt as if God spoke the words to me Himself through Jamie's book. The phrases kept building into a fuller picture, and I was gobsmacked. It didn't matter how far into *Worthy* I read, my heart was constantly being pierced. There were not only phrases I needed to hear to pull out roots but also statements to prune and refine me, to get me to question my true identity, to encourage me, and most of all to solidify that I was on the right path. God had a plan, just as he promises in Jeremiah 29:11 (NIV), "'For I know the plans I have for you,' declares the LORD, 'plans to prosper you and not to harm you, plans to give you hope and a future.'"

Here I thought God brought me to Spain so I could impact someone's life, yet He used the trip to impact me the most—to prove to me that I was worthy, that I deserved to be in Spain. I simply had to dissect my issues and commit to the necessary healing work so I could believe in myself, my worth, and fully receive the blessing He'd provided. I had no idea that my adventure in Spain would lead to the massive healing that took place, but I am so very thankful that it did. I will forever be grateful for the trip of a lifetime and what God provided for my self-worth.

After the healing of my self-worth in Spain, I knew my destiny. Lyrics from a familiar song entered my thoughts:

> I am chosen, not forsaken
> I am who You say I am
> You are for me, not against me
> I am who You say I am.[39]

What followed was a profound awakening. God used the following statements and phrases to confirm what He was already stirring in my heart.

> Just because your past didn't turn out how you wanted it to, doesn't mean your future can't be better than you ever imagined.[40]

> Where you are right now in your story matters less than the person you're becoming in it.[41]

> Don't forget, while you're busy doubting yourself, someone else is admiring your strength.[42]

> Your own knowing is more powerful than anyone else's advice. . . . Being willing to get knocked down and get back up again, and fail, and learn, and grow, is more powerful than waiting for someone to come into your life telling you what step to take next. . . . You have the power and everything you need inside of you right now to live the

highest, truest expression of yourself. . . .Your hard work and resilience are the path.[43]

When you have a vision on your heart, not everyone is going to get it. . . . God didn't give the vision to them, He gave it to you. . . . You are a steward of it. . . . Only you've been given the divine download, and now you are a steward of what to do with it. Of how strongly to believe in it. Of how willing you are to fight for it. Of how persistently you get back up every time you get knocked down. You are the owner. It's all in you, and it's all up to you.[44]

The ones who say, 'This doesn't make sense in my soul. I'm challenging that belief system.' They're the ones who help heal others, by first healing themselves. They're the ones who courageously share their ideas and offerings, no matter the criticism that might come.[45]

We can decide that what we fell victim to can be turned into victory for ourselves and others in part by helping others make it through those same painful things that we've now made it through. . . . We can decide if we turn our pain into purpose. And view our most challenging setbacks as setups in our lives, where we use what we went through, in the spirit of service and purpose, to now help others make it through too.[46]

You can tell I love powerful words. Please remember, your past does not define the ceiling of your future. It may have shaped you, but it does not own you. It does not disqualify you; it refines you. No past is beyond redemption. Even when your story has unfolded differently than you hoped, where you stand today matters far less than who you are becoming. Setbacks do not diminish you—they prepare you. When you choose to turn pain into purpose, you become living proof that healing does not end with survival; it multiplies through service. Your inner knowing is stronger than any outside opinion, and each time you rise after a fall, challenge a limiting belief, or choose truth over fear and healing over hiding, you are shaping the truest version of yourself. The strength you're doubting is already carrying you forward. Your worth was never lost—only waiting to be resurrected. God has proven, through my healing journey, that He uses the broken for something beautiful.

Healing does not end with restoration—it calls for responsibility. As God restored my heart, He taught me the importance of boundaries, not as restriction but as protection for what He had made whole.

Please scan the QR code to explore the songs that whispered hope—that beauty can rise from brokenness.

Chapter Eight

BOUNDARIES

Courage is simply the willingness to be afraid and act anyway.

—Robert Anthony

What does the word "boundaries" even mean? Do any of us really know what a boundary entails?

For years, my friends informed me that I needed to create boundaries. They raised concerns that I was enabling individuals in my life because I had not set much-needed boundaries. I will admit, I have not been good at creating boundaries and perpetually seem to overextend myself to do what is asked of me, all the while putting my own health and well-being at risk. The amount of stress and damage I have endured because of my lack of boundaries has taken years to restore. My liver, digestion, red blood cells, and mental health were in dire straits. The panic and anxiety attacks stress brought on is something I wish I had never had to endure.

However, apparently, I needed to learn the hard way with my health in shambles. Why? One simple word: fear. Fear of how I would be viewed if I said "no" and fear of not being accepted. It was not about becoming a superwoman and being able to accomplish challenging tasks; the problem lay in fear and the emotion of not feeling loved, so I continued to place my needs on the back burner while abusing my health. One thing I'll confess: I'd rather tackle any challenge and meet the deadline, no matter the cost, than ever say, "No, I can't." That's just how I am driven and who I was made to be—or so I believed.

I distinctly remember my counsellor stating that I needed to create healthy boundaries. I thought, *What on earth do healthy boundaries even look like?* How can we create healthy boundaries in our families when we naturally carry obligations, leadership, and responsibility for others? When our mind is constantly tracking everything that must get done, boundaries can feel selfish, unsafe, or even irresponsible. Yet, without them, the very things God has entrusted to us—our health, calling, relationships, creativity, and yes, resurrected worth—slowly get depleted. I wrestled with how I would be perceived (or slandered) and with the arguments I sensed were waiting on the horizon if I dared to implement boundaries for myself. Honestly, I dreaded the whole process and wanted to avoid the turmoil.

As I read further in *Worthy*, Jamie made powerful statements that explained the issue at hand.

> We're not wired to be happy, we're wired to be comfortable. . . . Even though we think we want to be happy, our subconscious drives us to do everything we can to get back to what's comfortable, a place that most accurately reflects our sense of worthiness.[47]

I recognized that being comfortable and keeping things the same were where I felt safe. To remove this comfort zone and all I had ever known was similar to asking me to climb Mount Everest; it seemed impossible. However, I was reminded that we need to have courage to succeed. "You can be comfortable or courageous, but you cannot be both."[48]

Healthy boundaries are limits we set to define our personal space, both physical and emotional, so we can protect our wellbeing and ensure healthy relationships. Boundaries include clearly communicating our needs and expectations while respecting the needs and boundaries of others.

I could not understand why I struggled so much with implementing boundaries until Jamie hit the nail on the head.

> Research shows inauthentic and even perfectionistic behaviors develop in childhood, when we learn to disregard our own wants and needs and become devoted to meeting the expectations and needs of others, in order to gain the feeling of belonging. We learn to hide the parts of us that don't earn praise and turn up the power on the ones that do. . . . These patterns leave us feeling empty,

disconnected, and ultimately unloved in the way we crave love most.[49]

What I read astonished me. I finally found the reason I struggled to create boundaries. The truth is, as a young child, my behavior was molded by what my father viewed as acceptable for him. I had to meet his expectations and needs to simply feel like I belonged or that I fit in.

Have you ever paused to ask where your own definition of "acceptable" came from—and whose expectations you've been living under? To stay in the "good books," of course, I would deny and hide parts of myself that wouldn't earn praise. I feared my father's temper. I hated it too. I prayed so often for God to take away his anger. Or that he would not come home from the road so I wouldn't have to be around his anger. I dreaded hearing the warning words from my mother: "Your father is on his way." Of course this makes complete sense. I was a powerless child seeking safety. Fear, without a doubt, drove *all* my actions. There was no question about it; I realized I could not say no or create boundaries because then I would have a sense that I didn't belong. My root of unworthiness started to sprout while I changed my behavior to fit in. What patterns did you absorb as a child that may still be silently directing the boundaries you struggle to set today?

I see now God had a specific plan with the roots He asked me to relinquish. He directed me in a strategic order for specific reasons. To recap what we've covered so far, I had to overcome my roots of anger, obedience, forgiveness, control, abandonment, rest, and worth. When I finally conquered the root of worth, the trajectory of my path significantly changed. I felt deserving and more confident than I ever had. If I had not pulled my roots out in this order, I do not believe I would have been able to keep pulling out the following roots. After I dealt with the words the Holy Spirit laid on my heart at each point in the journey, I revisited them with a healthy perspective and began creating much-needed boundaries.

After I returned from Spain, I found it quite simple to put myself first, something I'd wrestled with my entire life. I did not experience guilt for saying no, taking fewer clients, not doing all the chores around the yard and house. When I reflected and made a list of everything I would tackle in a day compared to the list my husband would, I sensed most of our household and family responsibilities were laid on me. I asked myself, *Why is this? How did I allow this to happen? Why can't Dave pick up the slack in some of these areas?* With this awareness, I began establishing healthy boundaries—discerning what I would and would not allow—so I could stop living in a state of constant overwhelm. Change showed up in practical ways: Dave and Raelyn occasionally did the grocery shopping, Dave took on more around the house, including cooking dinners, and he began taking Raelyn to appointments instead of working all day on the ranch and coming home expecting dinner to be waiting. Thankfully, farming is flexible, so I could ask him to implement these things without violating his boundaries.

With my new boundaries, I firmly viewed our marriage as a partnership, as a give and take where we both needed to join in raising and supporting our family. I began to see that this was not all mine to carry and that surrendering control in many of these areas was necessary—even when it meant releasing my preferences and expectations.

When we can clearly see that our worth lies in who God created us to be and how He views us, the pressure we place on ourselves to perform subsides. I finally felt as if I truly belonged and could take my rightful place as the child of God that I am. Boundaries naturally found their place in my life when I was able to find a healthy balance by prioritising my health and my healing.

As we anchor ourselves in worth, our emotional comfort zone expands, reshaping the friendships and relationships that feel familiar, safe, and desirable. I found it extremely hard to be in situations or around individuals who were constantly playing the victim or who chose to stay stuck on their own merry-go-round of negative patterns. How can we expect a different result when we are doing the same thing? We have to create a healthy boundary to protect our hearts and distance ourselves from this negative energy. As Proverbs 4:23 (NLT) declares,

> *Guard your heart above all else, for it determines the course of your life.*

My heart had shifted so deeply that I could now discern an unhealthy environment. I was determined not to allow myself to be drawn back into the same rut God had just freed me from. Paul reminds us of this in Galatians 5:1 (NLT),

So Christ has truly set us free. Now make sure that you stay
free, and don't get tied up again in slavery to the law.

Can you see who God created you to be buried beneath the layers you learned to wear? Are you willing to reconnect with your inner self and reclaim your worth? We are all created to be loved and to experience deep connection, yet many of us have learned to numb, disconnect, and survive without both. We were taught to grow up, be strong, push through, take care of everyone else, and keep moving—quietly labeling our deepest emotional needs as weakness. Freedom begins when you surrender the masks that kept you safe and trust God enough to step into who He always created you to be. You were never meant to survive your life—you were meant to live it fully, loved and whole.

Creating boundaries is uncomfortable. I knew I would get backlash from others, so I would rehearse both sides of those conversations beforehand. The more I allowed my mind to wander, the bigger the mountain seemed when in reality it was a molehill. I had to remember Jamie's statement, "Setting boundaries can feel like a betrayal to others. But not learning to is almost always a betrayal of yourself."[50] Sometimes creating boundaries means you will lose people in your life. If they don't stick by your side through thick and thin and allow you to be your true, authentic self, were they truly your friends to begin with? Sometimes we need to weed out those who bring us down and or use us. Living a life as your true, authentic self might be costly.

One of the hardest boundaries God asked me to implement required cutting off all communication with a family member. I knew the impact would ripple through the entire family, which made the decision all the more difficult. For months, I wept as this difficult task loomed over me. Responding in obedience, five months passed in silence as I cut off all communication. Then one day, the Holy Spirit prompted me clearly: *Pick up the phone and call.* Terrified, I dreaded making the call. I expected to hear the wrath of anger on the other end, but there was only calmness. I effectively communicated my boundaries, without apology—and something unexpected took shape. A new level of respect entered the relationship.

God may want us to create boundaries so He can work on both parties involved. It is phenomenal to witness how God works in the process when we are obedient and allow Him to do His work. Of course, this means we have to remove our fears from the equation and do as instructed. This is a hard concept to accept when I'm used to trying my hardest to correct all problems that lie in my path, but that is why He asked me to deal with my root of control before dealing with some of these others. We have to accept God's timing, not our own. We have to take a leap of faith and trust in the bigger picture. Every one of these shifts requires conscious effort and steady commitment.

As I became intentional about growing and deepening my relationships, I learned that honoring my capacity had to come first. Capacity itself became a boundary-setting tool that I implemented. Pausing to check my own capacity and allowing space for the other person to do the same created a sense of safety and mutual respect. This simple tool protected me from overgiving, self-betrayal, and emotional depletion, while still leaving room for genuine connection. It also taught me to be more intentional about how I value others' time, energy, and presence.

Does your mind race with a thousand unfinished thoughts, all competing for your attention? I know that race well—I lived there. But healing my worth changed that. As I reclaimed my worth, my mindset shifted, and now I prioritise my wellbeing above everything else. I will not apologize to anyone for "putting my oxygen mask on first" and taking care of myself. Remember, "The only people who get upset about you setting boundaries are those who are benefiting from you having none."[51]

Boundaries are the most impactful form of self-respect a person can have. I can certainly see why God asked me to work on mine. There is no better feeling in the world than knowing our worth, and boundaries helps us protect our worth. Just ask yourself, "Would you rather keep the peace around you or keep the peace within you?"[52]

What has the lack of healthy boundaries cost you? Do you feel undeserving of rest or taking time for yourself? What if I told you the limiting belief that you're not worthy of taking time for yourself is not true? The power our thoughts hold cannot be overstated. Own your worth. Speak life over yourself. Choose labels that strengthen and elevate your spirit. When you begin to value what surrounds you, as well as all that is within you, everything changes.

We only get one chance to be our true, authentic selves and live our best life. I encourage you to dig deep and make this life count. May you walk boldly and remove every barrier in your path—especially the one that tries hardest to hold us back: fear.

Please scan the QR code to listen to the songs that became my anthem as I stepped into new hope.

Chapter Nine

FEAR

I survived because the fire inside me burned brighter
than the fire around me.

—Joshua Graham

To say I had to process the root of fear is a vast understatement. 2 Timothy 1:7 (NLT) states,

For God has not given us a spirit of fear and timidity, but
of power, love, and self-discipline.

I believe we will *all* encounter fear at some point in our lives. A great number of us may have even suppressed fear our entire lives—perhaps fear of being alone, fear of not feeling safe, fear of not being enough, fear of feeling unloved, fear of failure, fear of rejection, fear of creating boundaries, fear of being hurt, fear of being ridiculed. You name it. I am sure that if we reflect on our lives and look deeper within, we will identify a root of fear.

Throughout my healing, I have uncovered the damage the emotion of fear caused in my life and relationships. Several of the fears previously mentioned found their place along the timeline of my life. The damage revealed itself as early as four years old. Fear creeps in when we least expect it to, and it will wreak havoc on our physical, emotional, and mental health.

On July 31, 2024, as I made my way to an appointment, I noticed a lot more traffic on the road than usual for that time of day. *Why are there so many vehicles?* I wondered. My "spidey senses" were engaged, and I was cautious! I kept my distance from vehicles approaching me or in front of me. Unfortunately, as I drove farther into town, I encountered another setback—one that would change my life as I knew it.

As I drove on an S-curve in the lane closest to the shoulder, I could see that the passing lane contained a string of vehicles traveling down the hill, but I had tons of room in front of me with no vehicles in my lane. Then, a sudden chain reaction unfolded ahead, forcing the vehicles beside me to slam on their brakes. In an instant, I was run off the road. From the corner of my eye, I saw a vehicle veer sharply into my lane, swerving to avoid the car in front of it. Right beside the vehicle as this happened, I quickly jerked my car to the right to avoid the impact. The next thing I remember, I was back in my lane, frantically crying, livid, and yelling at God. "What the hell?! Seriously?! Another flippin' impact?! Why not the vehicle in front of me? Why not the vehicle behind me? Why me again?!

You could stop this!" I felt targeted. This was not normal! Who in this world has four accidents in a short span of eighteen months, all at the hands of other drivers? I was convinced I was being targeted, but why? I phoned my sister-in-law and explained briefly what had happened, all the while hysterical. I asked her to call my mother, who was visiting me at the time, to come and pick me up because there was no way I could drive myself anywhere. She knew I was not healthy and that I was far from okay. As I continued to drive ever so slowly, liquid sorrow flowed down my face as I held my head with my left hand against the window in disbelief. I could not make sense of what I had just experienced. In shock, I crept down the hill, trying to reach the nearest intersection and get off the road.

Startled by a honk, I looked to my left. The driver who had veered toward me motioned for me to roll down my window, asking if I was okay. I replied, "No, I am far from okay." She pulled her vehicle beside mine in the nearest parking lot at the bottom of the hill. As she got out of her vehicle, the smell of marijuana followed her. I knew that her judgement was impaired, and sadly, I had once again paid the price for someone else's careless mistake. When I shared with her that I'd already suffered from PTSD and injuries from prior accidents, she felt awful. She continued to share that my defensive driving saved all their butts. That day, I should have been in a massive car pile-up or should have hit the cement barricade and light post, but praise God, I remained unscathed, physically (at least on the surface).

While I waited for my mother to arrive, I could sense the pattern in my body revving up all over again. I remained a mess—my nervous system trapped in a state of hypervigilance. I did not want to endure the months ahead and what this meant for my healing. The thought of what my future would hold was more than I felt I could bear.

As soon as I got home, I went straight to my room, wrapped my head with the medical device, and sobbed for hours as I fell asleep, wishing I were no longer on this earth. My mental state was rather dark, and I could not feel or see hope through recovery any longer. I was so angry and hurt, and frankly, I didn't understand why God was not answering my prayers for healing, but instead, He was allowing me to be buried alive with more trauma.

The following day, all my existing injuries flared. I didn't even know how to express myself anymore. I was consumed by anger toward everyone and everything, including God. For about a week, I was lashing out at God while on edge around my family. I could not understand why He'd allowed this to happen to me, again. Again! What was I missing? What had I not completed that He'd asked of me? Why was I invariably being punished? Life just did not make any sense, and I felt I had nothing left to give. I told Dave several times to dig a hole out back and end my misery. I was done fighting and trying; simply stated, I gave up.

While I continued in this wounded state, a dear friend called me to see how I was holding up. When I openly shared the darkness that embraced me, she immediately prayed with me. She kept speaking words of encouragement and told me God was with me and that He did protect me. I was baffled. *How is this God's way of protecting me?* I wondered. But, once again, I was reminded how Satan wanted to keep me down because of all the good I was doing for Christ. My friend continued to speak the name of Jesus over me, reminding me there was no room for Satan's schemes and that God is with me and helps me just as Joshua 1:9 (NLT) declares: "This is my command—be strong and courageous!

Do not be afraid or discouraged. For the LORD your God is with you wherever you go."

After I hung up the phone, I rested on the deck, gazing into nature while listening to "I Speak Jesus" by Charity Gayle and Steven Musso. The lyrics broke me.

> I just wanna speak the name of Jesus
> Over fear and all anxiety
> To every soul held captive by depression
> I speak Jesus.[53]

I pleaded with God while singing along in my brokenness. I started reflecting on the day of the fourth impact. I mulled over the smallest details that took place in the incident. I recall jerking the car to the right to avoid the impact, but the more I dissected every little detail, I realized I didn't turn the steering wheel left to get back on the road. I remember telling myself, "This can't be." I closed my eyes and replayed the event in slow motion, trying to remember precisely what had happened. Anything I may have missed? Over and over, I ran through the scenario. My curiosity was piqued; however, it was evident that God did protect me just as He declares in Psalm 121:7 (NLT), "The Lord keeps you from all harm and watches over your life." God guided my car back on the road when I didn't! The more I reflected on the speed I was traveling, the cement barricade two car lengths in front of me, the light standard, and traffic behind me, I realized there was no way I could have avoided a massive collision without an angel or God stepping in on my behalf.

I stared off into the trees, and my body became still as the reality sank in. Clearly, there could have been a lot more physical injury; however, the mental toll this took on me was by far the most severe injury up to this point. When I stepped into the knowledge of what God did to protect me, I knew He had a purpose during this storm. He would use this for His good as 2 Timothy 1:9 (NIV) proclaims, "He has saved us and called us to a holy life—not because of anything we have done but because of his own purpose and grace." Still, I just could not feel God through the darkness that surrounded me.

As the weeks went on, I continued to feel like an empty shell. One day I reclined on my zero gravity chair as I lay flat to relieve nerve pain while listening to the birds singing. My wind chime slowly soothed me as the leaves fluttered in the wind with the melody of the birds. Often I would look to the sky as if I were looking up to heaven and start talking to God. I could usually feel hope when I would do this, but this time it was different. This time, I could not feel hope as the darkness consumed me. I felt nothing, like a shell of myself. Fear had a tight grip on me, and I could not function in any state. I tried listening to different frequency tones and implemented EFT tapping as well as breathing techniques to help calm my nervous system—a daunting task after all my setbacks and a notably slow process, I have discovered.

Without a doubt, this was absolutely a dark part of my journey. I could not understand why God allowed me to experience severe mental illness on top of everything else. Why could I not catch a break? As I mentioned earlier, I strongly believe everything happens for a reason. This is a model I live my life by, and I needed to understand why this was happening to me. What was I missing? What was I supposed to learn? What was God's purpose in all I'd experienced and gone through?

Time passed, and I struggled greatly when around noise, people, or bickering. Like a wounded animal protecting itself, I isolated myself and took every opportunity to vanish. To my family, I'm sure it seemed as if I was avoiding them, and in essence, that was the truth. I struggled to live with myself during this phase of life and often sat alone, crying in disbelief at who I had become and what my life looked like.

A friend of thirty years flew up for a visit during August 2024, and she could see I was struggling with depression. She witnessed someone else taking up space in a person she once knew. As she shared her concerns with me, I cried and told her that I could sense something was drastically wrong. I was not the same person. I shared that if I could not pull myself out of it in the week to come, I would talk to my doctor about getting help. My family was not open to my taking medication for PTSD. We had seen how it had adverse effects on people in the family, changing them into people we no longer recognized. The fear of losing who I was sat at the forefront of my mind. The last thing my family or I wanted was to go down that road. My future looked bleak.

While I prayed about whether I should see my doctor and go on medication for PTSD, my intuition said that was not the answer. However, I went to my doctor and inquired about the next steps, as this feeling had lasted too long and grown stronger. At my appointment, the doctor prescribed a form of medication to help alleviate the PTSD symptoms. A few days after I started taking the medication, I had severe side effects, so the pharmacist advised me to stop taking it. I took that as my sign; this was not the road I was meant to travel. Internally, I felt I needed to stay the course and continue with prayer, my counselling sessions, and processing all the emotions involved.

During the next several counselling sessions, I sobbed. I felt so hopeless that the counsellor often asked me if I would harm myself. I could tell I was in a negative state with a feeling of nothing to live for. My comments were dark and hopeless, even though she would try to encourage me as we worked through past events. These sessions were profoundly different. In the past, I would have a setback for a few days or a week, but then I invariably rose above, ready to keep going. My resilience had been of stellar quality, but now, there was none. Even though I had help, I could sense myself slipping further and further into a dark pit. I grieved the life I'd once had. I felt all alone, that no one understood what I was going through, and most of all, I felt God had abandoned me.

Whenever I would drive, I became hypersensitive to vehicles within my bubble. If a vehicle approached too quickly toward a stop sign, I braced for impact; if a vehicle got too close to my lane, I braced for impact; if a vehicle cut me off, I braced for impact. I have had numerous close encounters where I have had to slam on my brakes to avoid an impact. I can plainly recall that I had to stop on Highway 16 due to construction. As I looked in my rearview mirror, vehicles were coming up too quickly for my liking. Fearfully, I kept saying, "I can't do this! They don't see me! They're going to hit me!" My mother laid her hand on my shoulder, saying, "We're okay; you got this; just breathe." She helped walk me through the panic.

My daughter has witnessed the same thing where I'm anxious and crying behind the wheel, physically not able to drive, and she has had to walk me through the panic or anxiety attack. She would place her hand on me and say, "Mom, just breathe, we got this, God is with us. You can do this!" Eventually, I would be able to get off the road, stop for a minute or so to try and compose myself, and breathe through the attack. Unfortunately, my mother and daughter were most often the witnesses of how anxious I would get behind the wheel as fear consumed the person they once knew. For someone who has ceaselessly been a good driver and not experienced a crippling fear like this, it felt devastating. I truly believe that unless you live through a similar experience, you simply cannot understand the crushing effects fear had on me.

With the hypersensitivity I experienced, my brain would scan everything for danger. As Jamie states, "If you believe something to be true about who you are, your brain scans and highlights proof around you that reinforces that belief."[54] I don't know if any of you have ever thought about buying a certain vehicle. Let's say you're looking at a new SUV, and all of a sudden you start seeing that SUV everywhere. It's not that these cars were not on the highway before, but that particular model is at the forefront of your mind so your brain is scanning your environment for that SUV, and you start seeing them everywhere. Well, because I became so fearful and focused on other vehicles hitting me, my brain was on high alert, constantly pointing out any hint of danger, which led to an extreme sense of exhaustion both mentally and physically.

Eventually, I could understand why my body responded with such a sense of survival and panic. Every single side of my vehicle had been impacted through the four accidents. Of course, I had a hard time riding in a vehicle; it no longer felt safe. As soon as I got behind the wheel, everything in me would tense up. If I saw poor road conditions or ice, my body would tense up. Whenever I was a passenger in a vehicle, my body would tense up as the lack of control intensified the situation, so I had to be the driver.

On September 6, 2024, while still struggling with the darkness that threatened to drown me, I decided that I would sign up for a subconscious mind course. The course intrigued me because it talked about "the power you hold to change your body, mind, and heart."[55] Before long I was deep in a four-day online course taught by Krystal. The concepts that appealed to me the most I share here.

New Paradigm: To help you get to better health

- Symptoms are a message from your body.

- Cultivate curiosity about your body and symptoms.

- Survival patterns formed by our environment and experiences can create symptoms.

- Your body is protecting you.

- We have an innate ability to heal and the body *wants* to heal.

Practical Tools for Immediate Use: You will be introduced to the "inner workings" of your mind and body. You will learn about

- Neuroplasticity—Change your brain to change your life

- Your survival brain—Your limbic system and your survival patterns

- Your autonomic nervous system—The greatest pharmacy in the world

- Epigenetics—Your DNA is not your destiny[56]

During this course, I discovered that certain things I felt and said to myself were all symptoms of survival mode. It's as if the light bulb finally went on and answers were illuminated. I now had the path God wanted me to take and understood that I had to reprogram my subconscious mind. I remember sitting Dave and Raelyn down and making them watch the "boring" video because it explained who I had become. I was not acting like a lunatic or being overbearing. I literally could not access 80% of my brain as it was offline. I needed them to understand I was merely stuck in survival and what that involved; I had not gone "crazy"; these were all real symptoms because of the physical state of my brain, and I could not help the way I acted. In fact, I was sick.

After I completed the course, I could see a glimmer of hope for the first time in a long time. I now had the tools I needed to start healing my brain. Krystal also taught about using the Tapping Solutions App for EFT tapping on the go. EFT Tapping has been a game changer for me and really helped me dive into uncharted territory for healing my subconscious. Tapping has become a daily routine for me and the tool I use the most.

Equipped with new tools, I started working on reprogramming my subconscious mind. The course taught me that I had to change my routine—things like sitting in a different chair at the dinner table, brushing my teeth with my left hand, taking a different route when I would drive, changing my passwords frequently, changing the screensaver on my phone, or moving furniture around in the house. I had to walk slowly as well because, if I rushed, it triggered my survival state and symptoms. So, needless to say, things looked different in our house for a while as I tried to create new neural pathways in my brain and rectify the damage that had been done. Essentially, I rewired my brain with new neural pathways so the old, fear-filled pathways would die off.

My counsellor had also taught me how to implement smells, if needed, to help pull me out of a heightened state. She explained that a strong scent would help bring me out of an attack—coffee, garlic, or just something pungent.

After days of feeling that the thick of the darkness was behind me, I asked my husband to drive us to church and instructed him to drive carefully and slowly, remembering I was in the vehicle. I felt hopeful and thought I could handle not being in control. Needless to say, I had officially become the worst backseat driver ever.

Unbelievably, we encountered a near-miss accident because of Dave's driving. Well, you can guess it, the PTSD flared immediately. When we arrived at church, I was panic-stricken and not able to function well. I stayed in the car tapping and praying in a frantic effort to calm myself, but I could not calm down amongst my tears. Nothing seemed to be working.

During our drive home after church, sadly, the atmosphere in the car shifted, turning so dire that I ended up yelling like a banshee at Dave. I came unglued, and the anger only grew stronger. Then, with the strength of rage, I backhanded him with my fist. My poor daughter watched in horror from the back seat, terror filling her eyes and emotion spilling down her face as she begged me to stop. She witnessed a person she had not seen before. I recall looking Raelyn in the eyes, seeing the frantic terror, yet "nobody was home" in my mind. Nothing registered, and I remained numb. At that moment, all I could say was that I fought with everything in me to survive. It was either Dave or me, and I proceeded to kick him out of the car during my fit of rage. This had not been the first time his driving had flared up my symptoms. This was about number five; his continued carelessness and lack of concern for my well-being had become more than I could or would tolerate.

You have to understand, it had taken about seven extremely rough weeks to crawl out of the depths of despair, and here the person who's supposed to love me and have my back was the one who contributed to my setbacks. I could not fathom how he could inflict more pain on me. I could not wrap my head around it. I could not function; I cycled in a state of panic and rage. By far, this is one of the most horrific memories I have of my healing journey. The damage this heightened extent of PTSD caused for me, my spouse, and my daughter has been life-altering and something I had to process heavily with counsellors in the months to come. I did not recognize who I had become. And how could I explain this to an eleven-year-old child?

It took weeks of therapy to work through the shame I felt in order to forgive myself. I know for certain that my actions and words during my journey have had lasting negative effects on my spouse, child, and marriage. Healing will need to take place for all of us, and I am fully trusting God to help restore our relationships. Sometimes I wonder if my responses throughout the years are why Dave shows a lack of care or concern. Regardless, the last thing I desire is to have this traumatic event affect the rest of my family's lives. I have lived through numerous traumatic events and know firsthand how it affects an individual if you do not seek help to deal with it.

Sometimes, forgiving someone is too hard; how can we forgive what we cannot forget? It may seem too hard, and it truly is. For me, each time the event sears my memory, being willing to hand the event and Dave to God over and over again, releasing both was the only solution. I've discovered that more often than not, forgiveness needs to be repeated. (Reference Chapter 3 if you need a reminder.)

Well, by now, I knew the drill. I embraced everything I needed to calm my nervous system, trusting that healing would come in time. It took about two weeks, and I eventually calmed myself to the point that I figured I'd be okay to venture down to Vernon, BC, on a business trip.

As I prepared to leave for Vernon, Dave decided to support me and come along. Trust me, I had learned my lesson, so I did all the driving. Later that evening, after we settled in at the resort, we got together with some of the business representatives. Within minutes, I was surrounded by three individuals who specifically said they needed to pray for me. A remarkably discerning individual asked me if I was the lady who'd had all those accidents. I said, "Yes, unfortunately, that would be me." He shared, "That is not normal. You know that, right? Satan's got a hold on you." This took me aback to hear what he said, yet I knew in my soul he might be on to something.

As one of the three individuals prayed over Dave and me, he shared that the strongman of fear was holding me captive and that Satan had used fear to keep me in bondage. They kept praying that the strongman of fear would be broken from me and that God would protect me, and specifically, that there would be no more fear as I drove. They covered safety, healing, our marriage, the ranch, and communication—specific things Dave and I needed to tackle. We prayed for about half an hour, and I felt different when we left. I could sense a shift, and now I knew for certain I was in the middle of a spiritual battle. A scripture that came to mind was 2 Thessalonians 3:3 (NLT).

But the Lord is faithful; he will strengthen you and guard
you from the evil one.

The next day at our training, one of my team members avoided me like the plague. By the end of the day, I discovered that she had sabotaged me, tried to destroy my reputation, ruin my friendships with business colleagues, ruin my business, and keep me down with spiritual forces involved. I'll be the first to admit I do not fully understand how the power of spiritual warfare manifests itself, but I assure you it is real. As I thought back to how I met this team member and the things that were said along the way, something just did not sit right with me. I believe in my soul she was involved with putting the strongman of fear into me. Instantly, I had a memory from a trade show I had take part in. This team member had a lady who ran a booth of crystals and fortune telling come and use the medical device, and an hour later, she came back sitting on my device again. Astonished, I said, "This is not allowed. You can only use it twice a day, several hours apart. You had your session, and I need you to leave." The way she got off the chair so quickly and vanished to her booth was similar to how demons respond when Jesus is speaking directly to them in the movies. I believe at that moment God or an angel spoke through me.

As I kept putting the pieces together, I knew I was under heavy spiritual attack, which explained why I had such a hard time breaking free from the grip of fear. I began to feel similar to Job in the Bible, especially the part where God allowed Satan to test his faithful servant, as explained in Job 1:12 (NLT).

> *"All right, you may test him," the Lord said to Satan. "Do whatever you want with everything he possesses, but don't harm him physically."*

To my amazement, as we headed home, I handled driving really well. Even though I came across an incident where I had to suddenly slam on the brakes and veer off to the shoulder, I was able to change the narrative in my mind. Oh, the thoughts were instantly there, trust me. They came with a vengeance! "I'm going to get hit!" My heart was in my throat, but then I said to myself, "We got this, just breathe, we got this." A minute later, I felt good to go as if nothing had happened. I was so impressed! It had been a long time since I could drive in this fashion. I felt as if the barrier of fear was finally removed, and it was time to get back on track with my healing journey. While I am not saying spiritual warfare is at the root of all fears, I encourage you to consider how and why fear may be manipulating you.

After I got home from my trip to Vernon, I started reading a book called *Attacking Anxiety: From Panicked and Depressed to Alive and Free* by Shawn Johnson.[57] While I was reading through the book, several thoughts struck a chord. "You are not crazy. You are not alone. This will end."[58] This became my new mantra and gave me hope. The further I read, the more I understood that I am not alone in my feelings, that many of us suffer in silence. *Attacking Anxiety* has been a valuable healing piece for my mental health, and I strongly encourage anyone who is struggling with depression, anxiety, or panic attacks to read it.

Shawn brought me back to three grounding truths: to look back at all God had already brought me through, to stand firm in what He had promised, and to trust that He is with me every step ahead.

When anxiety or depression weighs heavily and our cries to God seem to echo back in silence, hope can waver. Unanswered prayers can tempt us to believe God is distant or indifferent to our cries. Yet God is never absent. Silence is not stillness. God is always at work, moving every piece toward a greater good.

I had to remember the truths God promises.

> God is with you—even if you can't feel it.
> God is working—even if you can't see it.
> God has a plan—even if you can't understand it.[59]

As my counselling sessions continued, I would often refer to my progress as my position on the mountain. I visualized myself climbing up a mountain, and with the numerous setbacks I'd encountered, it seemed I would likely not make it to the top. Every time I made it two-thirds of the way up the mountainside, a setback of some sort ended up kicking me down the slope. I visualized myself near the bottom of the mountain when this would happen, having to start the climb all over again. The image of climbing the mountain has stuck with me ever since, with my goal being to finally make it to the top one day. Although I will admit, I had my doubts I would ever get there. The journey took forever, and I got weary.

A few months after processing all of the fear I'd faced and feeling as if the worst was behind me, I headed on a road trip to southern British Columbia and Alberta. Impressed with my driving skills, I could not believe the progress I had made. I was better than okay! I did awesome behind the wheel, even with people cutting me off or coming into my lane. I thought, *How marvelous,* as I thoroughly enjoyed every minute with no fear.

Then, on May 25, 2025 . . . I had the privilege of making my way up Sulphur Mountain in Banff, Alberta, lifted 7,486 feet into the air by gondola. I love mountain-top views and was excited as I stood in line waiting for my turn. As I entered the four-person gondola, I was seated on one side with a couple across from me. The door closed, and we were off. We proceeded over a T-bar connection, and the gondola started to swing. Instantly, I was filled with fear. I experienced trembling, sweating, anxiety; my heart raced, I felt nauseous, and I had to close my eyes. I kept imagining the gondola falling off the cable to the earth below and me dying.

As the gondola climbed farther up the steep mountain, I remained incredibly still, searching for something to brace myself against but finding only the rod at the back of the seat. I gripped the seat with all my might, bracing for the inevitable. Every slight rocking sensation I endured heightened my fear. I sensed a severe panic attack taking hold, and I had no idea how I was going to make it to the top of this mountain. After all, my journey had just begun. I started praying, begging God for protection the entire way while frantically trying to hold it together in the gondola. We were climbing at what seemed like a snail's pace, and the trip took far too long; I didn't know if I could hang on.

Finally, I made it to the top! I thought of searching for first aid because I was *not* okay. I could not stop shaking, and panic attack symptoms were in full swing. I did not know how on earth I was going to be able to ride the gondola to get back down. I phoned my sister-in-law from the top of the mountain, asking her to pray, and she reminded me to use all my tools. The prospect of descending the mountain was so terrifying that I reached out to several people and asked them to pray for me as I proceeded to make my way to the restroom so I could start tapping. There, in the stall, amongst the sorrow, I made my own tapping phrases for the first time to try to calm my nervous system. While tapping on the nine meridian points, I kept saying, "God is with me; He is here right beside me; God will protect me; there is no room for fear; you are safe." I prayed for God to give me peace and strength to make it down the mountain in one piece. About forty minutes later, as I stood in line to take my seat on the gondola, I had settled quite a bit, but some fear still lingered. I kept praying for His peace that passes all understanding and saying, "God is with me. We got this!"

As my turn came, lo and behold, I was the only one in the gondola on the way down. I sat on the back side so I could view the mountains (in case I was able to look) while I made my way down. As soon as the door closed, I felt peace. Suddenly, I had a visual of Jesus sitting right beside me with His arm around me, saying, "We got this!" a familiar phrase He had told me in a vision while working through my triggers with Christ-Centered EFT tapping. An incredible amount of peace rushed over me; it truly is unexplainable.

I don't even know how to explain the difference those forty minutes of bathroom stall prayers made. I know for certain the power of prayer, and God does lift up those who are in need. Prayer works. Regardless of having experienced this several times throughout my journey, I was once again amazed. I moved around in the gondola, took pictures, and remained "cool as a cucumber." A complete 180 from the girl who went up the mountain. Later that evening, while reflecting on what had happened, a powerful quote entered my thoughts: "The best view comes after the hardest climb."[60]

Shortly after I got home from Alberta, I had a meeting with my counsellor. I shared the gondola experience and the fear that was still present. I did not know if I needed to work through something I'd missed or why it had happened. She shared with me that she knew exactly why I went through it. I felt perplexed; *how could she know this?* She explained that for two years, I had visualized myself climbing up a mountain while enduring endless setbacks that kicked me down to the beginning. It made complete sense to her that I remained terrified of falling to my death, fearing I would not make it up the mountain. She said I physically climbed the mountain I'd envisioned and that I'd anticipated the familiar setback was about to happen. The tension and fear were remarkably real as I braced for impact, and the only impact I saw was falling to my death. Furthermore, she shared that what is even more incredible was the peace I felt coming down the other side of the mountain. This solidified that I *will* make it to the top, and God *will* meet me there when I do. Wow! That was deep. I pondered all her wisdom and knew she had hit the nail on the head. After all, "If it doesn't challenge you, it doesn't change you."[61]

God has proven to me time and time again that He keeps showing up in places I least expect Him but most need Him.

Fear is scary, and I, of all people, understand how paralyzing its effects are; being released from the grip of fear is an incredible experience.

I encourage you to reflect on the following questions that I had to ask myself as I processed my root of fear.

- What has fear cost you in your life already?

- Are you shrinking yourself to feel safe?

- Are you dimming your soul's light to stay comfortable or hidden?

- Are you willing to meet fear face-to-face and challenge its grip on you?

- Are you willing to clothe yourself with the courage you need to break free from fear?

Remember:

> The devil has come to steal, kill, and destroy. Jesus has come to give you life abundantly. Ask God to show you the truth about your situation. Don't let the enemy of your soul talk you into accepting anything less than what God has for you.[62]

Once we can face our fears, value our worth, and accept our true identity, we can live as our true, authentic selves. That, my dear, is when the magic happens. But authenticity has a way of exposing what still hurts. As we step into our truth, things unsettle us and our triggers begin to surface, inviting deeper healing.

Please scan the QR code to listen to the songs that carried my heart's cry while God healed my root of fear.

Chapter Ten
TRIGGERS

*Resilience is a choice. It's choosing to rise above your circumstances,
no matter how difficult, and become the person you're meant to be.*

—David Goggins

I must say I never thought of triggers having an effect on my physical health. In fact, I did not think of triggers at all until God insisted I dig out my root of triggers. Yes, I may have lived under a rock in the past, I know! However, I did not have the knowledge of how triggers impacted me, so I investigated to gain further wisdom.

I learned that emotional triggers are people, places, situations, or experiences that ignite an intense—often disproportionate—emotional response rooted in past experiences, trauma, or unresolved wounds. These triggers can be activated by specific words, sounds, smells, familiar faces, or even internal thoughts. They may operate consciously or subconsciously and often set off the body's natural fight-or-flight response. When triggered, individuals may experience intense emotions like fear, anger, or sadness, and their reactions can range from panic to withdrawal and overwhelm.

As I reflected on the explanation of emotional triggers, it became clear that I needed to continue working through my trauma. The biggest hurdle I was about to face, unbeknownst to me, waited in the wings. As I began learning to identify my triggers, a revelation emerged that blew me away. Never in my wildest dreams would I have anticipated what God revealed.

Remember the cautionary note from my author's note—some of the memories I'm about to share are gut-wrenching and may be difficult to read. If you are currently in a state of overwhelm, I encourage you to approach this chapter with care, as it could be triggering. Perhaps even skip over this chapter; return if and when you choose or are able.

As I processed significant memories, some were incredibly vivid, as if I'd traveled back in time. Often, as I would think about the memory, my emotions would start flowing, and before long, I knew the trigger and how it impacted my everyday life and current health struggles. During my sessions, I tackled triggers directly as well as my emotions attached to the memory. It was a painful process of releasing long-buried emotions—feelings that had quietly eroded my health and molded the person I had become. Sometimes, I had to visit these memories multiple times if I wanted to release the different layers of trauma associated with them. It was not just a "one and done" process.

I have chosen to share a few memories from my counselling sessions to provide further insight into how the healing process came to fruition.

The Escape

My eyes were closed, and as I took deep breaths, the counsellor gently guided me into being present within my body. I could feel the chair beneath me and my breath flowing deeper throughout. Then, a specific memory surfaced. I was nine years old and playing with a friend in my bedroom while my father struggled to repair the furnace in our trailer. I was about to walk through my bedroom door into the hallway when suddenly my father had a fit of rage. Next thing I knew, a knife flew down the hallway in my direction. I froze! This event caused an immense amount of fear, shame, embarrassment, and humiliation, and I literally felt trapped. I had no words for my friend as we looked at one another, but I knew that no one would ever want to come to my house again because of my father's actions.

As I remembered the event, several emotions washed through my body. I could visualize myself at *that* specific age with *that* particular friend in *that* environment. Amid the fear and tears of processing this event, my counsellor asked me to create a way to escape that bedroom. Suddenly, I could visualise a window I could climb out of. It was not safe for me to exit the house any other way, so I snuck out the window. As I managed to escape, I frantically ran deep into the forest that surrounded our trailer, through the tall poplar trees where no one would find me. When I thought I had run far enough away, I stopped.

Right then and there, my counsellor asked me to say what I needed to say to my father. She assured me I needed to release how I felt and to let it all go so I could move forward. With that permission, the anger and grief I had suppressed erupted in a scream that came from the depths of my soul. Everything I wanted to say to my father poured out of me. Specific phrases were, "Why can't you control your anger? Why do you constantly want to hurt us? How could you embarrass me like this? I do not feel any love from you, Dad; I only feel pain." As I continued to process the memory and release built-up emotions, I could feel a shift throughout my body. It appeared my emotions were on the move. Then, the counsellor gently guided me back to the present as I opened my eyes and wiped away the moisture.

She asked me how I was after what had just occurred. I replied that discomfort rose from my legs all the way into my back and shoulder area, and I felt really sad. After processing a major event that I had stored within me for a long time, I usually felt physically better for the rest of the day as the pain in my body subsided quite a bit. However, this time, the following few days were rough as I felt intense pain present in different areas of my body—pain I did not see coming and that rattled me.

Longing to Be Held

As the counsellor guided me deeper within my body, I closed my eyes. I could detect warming sensations, sometimes a light breeze, and before long, the memory would appear. I was about five years old. I had asked my parents to pierce my ears and received a harsh "no." Other girls in school had earrings, and I wanted to fit in. I wanted to feel pretty and important. So I took one of my mother's earrings and decided to pierce my own ear with it.

The earring had a tiny ball on the top with a faint pink heart attached to it. I felt pleased that soon I would be able to wear this beautiful gem. I looked into the bathroom mirror, held a potato behind my earlobe, and started the process of piercing my own ear. Trying with all my might to push the earring through my earlobe, I nearly fainted. Multiple times, I had to lie down on my bed or go outside to get some air to relieve the queasiness. With determination, I stood back in the bathroom, staring into the mirror, attempting once again to get the job done. The process took a few hours, but I persevered and didn't give up. I don't recall how long it took exactly, but I do remember it was not quick. Eventually, when I pushed the earring through, it sat near the bottom of my ear, not where it should be placed. Regardless, I remained incredibly proud of myself and excited that I could wear this tiny heart earring. Well, soon enough, my mother found out. How naive I was to think she would not notice. I knew I could not hide this from my father, either, and I recall my mother warning me, "You wait till your father gets home." A phrase I feared with everything in me.

Then, my father arrived. I saw myself watching the memory from a distance while in the same room, like in the movies when the soul leaves the body. I was sitting in front of him on the ground as he swiveled on a flowery chair in the living room. Sarcastically, he asked me if I had any brains. As he got more aggressive with his words, I recall being yelled at, and I braced myself. I hated being yelled at; that punishment was enough and broke my heart. In a threatening voice, he said that if I wanted earrings that badly to give him a pair of scissors. He would stab them through my ears and make me some. Frantically crying in fear, I begged to be spared. I could see my whole body start trembling with terror and emotion as I watched this memory. Such an innocent desire to fit in and feel pretty or special, he turned malignant while threatening me.

The counsellor then asked me what I was feeling. My body became rigid, trembling inside while furious on the outside. I could see the five-year-old version of myself with blonde pigtails, wearing a bright pink shirt and pants. The counsellor asked me where the older version of myself stood, and I responded, "On the side of the room watching." She asked me to ask the younger version of me what she needed. Vividly in my mind, the five-year-old ran to the older me, and I swept her in my arms. "She wants to be held," I replied.

As I held her, I could visualize and feel the little girl tightly wrapping her arms around my neck, as if she were hanging on for dear life, while resting her head on my shoulder as she wept. As the minutes passed, several times the counsellor asked me what was happening. I replied, "I am just holding her, and she is still crying." We stayed in this memory for probably five to eight minutes at least. After a long while of silence, the counsellor asked me again what the little girl felt. I replied, "She's just so sad; she's heartbroken. She wants to be held for a while." I stayed in this memory a while longer until the little girl lifted her head off my shoulder with a big smile on her face and asked me if she could go outside and play. "Of course," I responded as I released the embrace. As I watched out the front window, the little girl ran happily outside to her bike as if nothing had taken place.

As the counsellor guided me back to the present, I was exhausted and sad, yet I felt a shift. It is a remarkable process, and I don't even know how to express the feelings I experienced. I told my counsellor that I found it interesting that the five-year-old version of myself wore pants and ran outside immediately to her bike. This explains a lot about who I am today and why my Harley-Davidson is my go-to. I shared that she felt a sense of freedom on a bike, where no one could control her, and that wearing pants gave her the confidence to flee if she ever needed to.

After all these years, a truth finally surfaced. Processing this memory became a pivotal point; it shed light on the reasons behind many of my choices and reactions in life. Another takeaway I discovered was that I long to be held. Dave's workaholism triggers this deep longing. The memory revealed a wealth of knowledge and shed a spotlight on some of my deeper struggles.

Lashings

I closed my eyes, took deep breaths, and could feel the air within my torso, almost like a slight fluttering feeling. As I began to settle, another memory appeared. I don't recall exactly how old I was, but I'm guessing around ten. I stood in the room watching from the sidelines as the memory started to play out.

It appeared I was in trouble with my father for lying. Lying was something he didn't tolerate, and being lied to became a trigger I had to process. I remember being bent over the brown dining room chair as he took his leather belt and proceeded to yell at me to never lie again while spanking me. His spankings were no ordinary spankings; they were more to beat me into submission. My cries and pleas went unheard; through tears and pain, he continued until my young body bore the marks of his anger. I watched in disbelief as my mother stood by, allowing this to happen to me.

After retreating to my room, I stared into the mirror, desperate to understand the agony. The sight of the red, swollen marks on my body brought sorrow and a surge of anger I could not contain. Over time, they darkened into a remarkable mix of deep purple with hints of blue and yellow. For days, I could hardly sit because of the pain I experienced. The counsellor asked me what I wanted to say to my father. I replied, "I want to grab that belt and whip him with it." She told me to take the belt from him and to tell my father everything I needed to say.

In my vision, I saw myself repeatedly hitting my father as hard as I could as he stood against the wall in the dining room. I yelled, "How does it feel now?! How does it feel when you have no control and someone doesn't stop?!" For minutes, I kept hitting my father with everything in me. During this vision, I saw that my father looked at me, speechless, raising his arms to defend himself. He appeared startled but didn't say one word.

Eventually, my counsellor had to guide me back to the present because I was not stopping. Built-up anger exploded out of me, every trauma and suppressed emotion I had carried at his hands releasing through that belt. Again, she asked me how I felt, and I simply stated, "Emotionally drained." However, as the day went on, I noticed a shift in the physical pain. Then, the same routine would follow. The next few days, a lot of discomfort took hold in my body as emotions were released from different areas.

As I worked through this trigger with the counsellor's help, I quickly sensed its link to control, safety, and a helpless feeling where I remained silent. I did not have a voice. This was a new realization—one which explained why I would not allow anyone to control anything about me when I became an adult. At the age of seventeen, I moved out of my childhood home and bought my first house. I would rather be broke making mortgage payments than living under my father's roof. My challenger spirit worked overtime to keep me safe. Not only that, but when I felt as if I was not being heard by those close to me, this triggered a deep emotion from within. I could see how I struggled with this trigger almost daily, especially with relationships. I am so thankful that I got to the bottom of this trigger and processed it so that I could see a path forward. I knew something within me had changed—I could feel a shift in my heart that would shape how I responded in the future.

Shortly after these sessions, I felt God leading me to reach out to a practitioner who offered Christ-centered emotional freedom technique (CC-EFT) sessions. I had a strong sense that the Holy Spirit would guide her into specific areas I needed to process.

Christ-centered EFT is a healing method that combines tapping techniques with prayer, inviting the Holy Spirit to guide the process of releasing emotional wounds and restoring inner peace.

Ready to trust God, I wanted to try a familiar technique, tapping, with a more meaningful approach to my healing. I needed her specialized techniques so I could get to the bottom of my triggers, perhaps even to access memories I'd blocked.

At my first meeting with the practitioner, she shared that a traumatic event around the age of five is where we needed to start. Her sessions are powerful and truly remarkable. They took me into a new dimension to heal; however, I was still self-aware and willing, not hypnotized. I have chosen to share a few highlights from my sessions.

Traumatic Event

I closed my eyes as she started to guide me. Before long, the memory became present. As with the other sessions, I watched from within the room as the scene played out before my eyes. I appeared to be around four years old at the time, and I can remember every detail about the traumatic event.

It all started while my family attended a barbecue gathering with my parents' friends. It was late at night and dark. My father had been drinking and started arguing with my mother. Next, my siblings and I were being yelled at to get in the car as my father continued to spew in rage. As we were driving home, he went extremely fast down the gravel roads, so much so that I got butterflies in my stomach when going through intersections. There was a lot of anger and yelling.

When we made it home, I saw my father pin my mother against the wall in the hallway of our house as he screamed at her, accusing her of something. Several threats were yelled in anger. My father threatened to kill all of us if my older brother didn't learn how to shoot a gun. My older brother was only seven at the time. Fearing for my life, I took my younger brother, and we hid under one of the beds as far against the wall as we could, hoping my father would not find us.

As I watched the memory, my heart broke, and a waterfall of sorrow poured down my face. I could see that the four-year-old me shook in terror, fearful for her life. It appeared I was also protecting my younger, two-year-old brother, whom I had hidden behind me. Breathing seemed almost too loud as I tried with everything in me to be invisible. Violence thundered through the hallway. I clamped my eyes shut, desperate to escape the noise. That's when I froze!

The practitioner asked me to open my eyes and to look around the room and find the specific color she mentioned. Next, she guided me through CC-EFT to release the emotions while creating a new narrative amongst the pain and emotion. She then asked me to revisit the memory, but this time, there were small changes. She asked me to bring Jesus into the room with me. As I closed my eyes and visually brought back the scene, I could see Jesus near the place where the older version of myself stood. Jesus had His hand reached out toward my younger self, but I could not move. I looked at Him but I felt too traumatized and fearful. I did not want to come out from under the bed. I did not trust people, and I feared for my life. I was not safe.

Every time a new emotion would surface amid the pain and anguish I felt, she would guide me to open my eyes and look at a specific color in my room as she led me through a new narrative using CC-EFT. Sometimes she guided me to place a specific emotion in a blessing ball of light that I envisioned Jesus holding in His hands as He raised it to the sky to release the emotional attachment to the memory. I processed several rounds similar to this until no further emotions surfaced. It took a lot of gut-wrenching, painful work to process this particular memory amongst the emotions I experienced. More than I ever cared to endure, that's for darn sure.

Finally, I looked up from under the bed, and I could see Him. The man who appeared before me wore a long white robe with a tan sash around His waist. His long brown hair was neatly tucked behind His ears. I reached for His hand—Jesus's hand—as He gently pulled me out from under the bed. He held me in His arms and assured me that I was now safe. Love radiated from Him, and He was incredibly kind, something I had not experienced before from a man. Every space in the room filled with an incandescent glow. Even though I could see the image of my parents in the hall and see the four-year-old version of myself under the bed, I could no longer sense the emotions that were attached or hear the noise. The emotions that haunted me about that memory seemed to vanish as I released them to Jesus.

That's when the practitioner asked me if a color had entered the room. Sometimes the color would appear as a fog, and the room would start filling from the bottom with white. Sometimes hints of yellow, blue, or pink appeared as well, as I focused on Jesus being in that room and filling it with love and peace.

During this process, I allowed Jesus's love and peace to fill my heart and remove the negative feelings. I started looking through a lens that He provided. After I released this horrific memory, it cemented why I had a root of control with so many triggers. I literally froze in survival programming from this traumatic event and had lived my entire life without knowing any different. The freeze response is "a physical reaction to extreme fear or trauma. It is activated when we have lost all hope of fighting off or fleeing from a dangerous situation." This explained why I have struggled so much. All my trials appeared to be side effects of survival programming and keeping myself safe. All I wanted as a young child was to feel safe and to feel loved. Something I continuously longed for but that remained out of reach until Jesus saved me and embraced me in that moment.

Another realization that came from this session was how obligated I felt to protect my younger brother. Due to this obligation, creating boundaries with my brother became a struggle. Once I was able to process all my emotions and triggers with this memory, I no longer felt that obligation. It was not my responsibility to protect him. It never was, but at four years old, I didn't know any different.

Nothing compares to how loved I felt when Jesus held me tight in His arms after coaxing me out from under the bed. Reframing my limiting beliefs around this trauma took a bit of work, but I constantly reminded myself that all "difficult roads lead to beautiful destinations."

Dumpster Girl

As I entered another session, I closed my eyes and got comfortable within my body. I felt my breath within, and the practitioner gently guided me with a few words until I had a vision. In this particular vision, I saw a haggard-looking and curly-haired girl. She was in a darker location with wrappers, food, and bugs stuck everywhere. She wore stained, tattered clothes, almost like rags, and appeared to be a complete disaster. At first glance, I could not recognize who she was. The practitioner asked me, "Who is she?" I pondered for a while until it came to me. Then, it hit me, this was me!

Honestly, I looked as if I'd fallen out of a dumpster and lived on the streets my entire life. This vision led me to understand that I punished myself and kept myself in bondage because of how I viewed myself. My subconscious viewed me as this image! Worthless. Rejected. What a sobering vision. All the negative remarks I have said or heard held me in this image as I wore the layers of filth I'd placed upon myself. Complete shock overtook me. I realized I didn't think highly of myself, hence the reason I had self-worth issues, but I had no idea it had evolved to this extent. The image of that dumpster girl is a horrific thing to witness.

With the practitioner's help, I was able to process the layers of why I viewed myself this way. As I started removing layers of emotional pain, I was able to dig deeper into the root. She shared that "most root issues are lies you are believing about the situation and your identity." I also discovered that not once did I feel worthy of anything. This includes people's time, love, respect, and especially God's love and forgiveness. Internally, I felt like a doormat constantly being stepped on and put down.

After my session, a word I had heard from a trusted counsellor came to my mind: *shame*. I can still hear her saying, "There is no room for shame" as she prayed over me. She reminded me that I had done nothing wrong, yet I felt so much toxic shame that I viewed myself as the dumpster girl.

Soon after, a memory surfaced from a women's retreat I had attended. Elisha Rose spoke about her book, *I Am Worthy*, and something she said caught my attention. "Fear does not hold us hostage of our worth, *shame* does." There was that word shame again. Elisha further shared, "We feel shame because we are avoiding the truth."

I knew the truth was buried beneath the pain, so I dared to go deeper than I ever had before. Depending on how emotional I was, the color I looked at during my session would vary. However, all the power the emotion held in the memory diminished using her specialized techniques. Other times, I pictured myself taking back the keys I had once handed to someone who held power over me, in particular, my father and my husband. Taking back the keys from them was symbolic of taking back my value, which helped me further accept my worth. This was a necessary step so I could create healthy boundaries and restore the years of damage that had occurred.

The trigger of shame did not just stir emotions—it detonated years of suppressed pain, exposing layers of hurt I did not even know were rotting inside me. It revealed deep wounds that God invited me to confront, heal, and finally release. Confronting the trigger of shame was difficult because it forced me to believe in myself—something I had struggled to embrace for so long. I had to believe that I am enough. That I am worthy of love. That my life could be different. I had to change my limiting beliefs and accept that I am a child of God, created in His image as Genesis 1:27 (NIV) states, "So God created mankind in his own image, in the image of God he created them; male and female he created them." I had to accept who God told me I am. Reframing the negative thought patterns that my subconscious had stored was not effortless, and it took time to rebuild. Nothing happens overnight. If shame were stripped of its power in your life, what freedom, identity, and peace might finally rise in its place?

My Secret Place

I remember the practitioner sharing that I would access my secret place. I had no idea what that meant. As I closed my eyes, she asked me to envision an escalator going up into my heart, and then the door of my heart would open so I could step inside. Suddenly, I could picture myself as the five-year-old girl riding on the escalator that appeared like a steep mountain as it climbed high to the top. A red glow surrounded me. As I got to the top and crossed the doorway, I saw a spectacular view.

I had been taken back in time: the street was made of cobblestone, while the edges were lined with rustic wooden tables heaped with fresh fruit and vegetables. People appeared happy, laughing and mingling while wearing long robes of all sorts of colors. Bright colors caught my attention. The gardens and flowers were lush and their hues vibrant, full of life. *Beautiful! Simply beautiful*, I thought. On the right side of my vision, I saw a paved walking path edged by medium-sized brush and sandhills. I stood in the middle of the market, with blonde ringleted hair, while wearing a breathtaking white dress.

The practitioner asked me if I could see Jesus anywhere in my secret place. I replied that I could see Him walking down the paved pathway toward the market. Instantly, I ran in His direction, waiting to be embraced. I was so excited, running as quickly as my little legs could go, full speed into His arms. With a big smile, He asked me, "How are you today?" I replied, "I am sad." He asked me why I was sad, and I said, "I don't feel loved." Jesus looked directly in my eyes and told me I was loved more than I would ever know. As He held my hand, we walked along the path, smiling, talking, and laughing.

Before I left my secret place and the precious vision that had appeared, the practitioner asked me to see if Jesus wanted to tell me anything else. Then I heard Him tell me, "Go and make disciples." He made it clear that I am to empower and inspire. I love His guidance, pure medicine healing a broken heart.

Numerous times, before I could process my triggers, I accessed my secret place. I'd see the market, and happiness surrounded me as everyone acted so kindly. Then, Jesus and I would walk down the paved pathway. Some visions were of us sitting on a high sandy hill with sparse bushes overlooking a stunning beach in front of a large body of water. We conversed like best friends, chatting about anything and everything. As I brought up heartfelt concerns about my physical healing, quite often Jesus would look at me and say, "We got this!" It was the same image and phrase I had seen and heard in the gondola riding down Sulphur Mountain after my panic attack. The same phrase I had to say multiple times behind the wheel as panic threatened to overwhelm me while I drove.

One time, the practitioner asked me what I noticed as I looked around my secret place, and I responded, "Everyone is happy; there is no sadness; there is no sorrow." I loved that because I felt joyful. I remember playing with toys in the market and having a superb time, just so pleased to be there. I asked her "Why am I invariably the little five-year-old girl, and why am I unfailingly wearing a white dress?" She explained that this was the season when most of the damage had occurred and when my heart had most desperately needed to feel loved. The white dress represented my innocence. I was a precious child and needed to feel that I mattered. Until I could fully release all the emotions hindering this healing stage and replace them with positive, empowering ones, this image would keep appearing. This was incredible information, absolutely life-changing. Eventually, I was able to replace the negative memories in my subconscious with positive memories from my secret place.

In another session, as I entered my secret place after processing the dumpster girl vision, I saw a bright light coming toward me. At first glance, I thought it was my guardian angel. As she got closer, the first thing I noticed was that she was not wearing glasses. She stood half my size, had long hair, and she wore a long maroon-colored dress with a long vest over it. I could not place who she was, but with the practitioner's guidance, I soon grasped that it was the soul version of myself. The version that I am supposed to live my life as. This image is the complete opposite of the dumpster girl. I felt completely rattled by what surfaced.

The Holy Spirit also instructed the practitioner that "Constance doesn't know who she is yet." That phrase has stuck with me. Sometimes, I wonder if He is talking about my place as a child of God or something more profound. From that conversation, I decided to start living my true, authentic life as the child of God that I am.

While processing my triggers, several layers would surface, layers I did not even know existed. There were days when I felt completely drained and needed God to carry me through because I simply didn't have the strength. During those times, I had to remind myself of the words of Mary Anne Radmacher: "Courage doesn't always roar. Sometimes courage is the quiet voice at the end of the day saying, 'I will try again tomorrow.'"[63]

My homework during these sessions was to access my secret place daily or a few times per week so I could create a positive habit. Whenever I felt overwhelmed or in the trenches, I would close my eyes and go up that escalator into heaven on earth within my heart, a place where I could be alone with Jesus, where time stood still, and nothing else mattered except for what He would tell me and what I would see.

Are you willing to take personal responsibility and transform your health? The choice is yours: continue ignoring the hidden roots of your stress and the physical symptoms they produce, or surrender it to God, and allow Him to heal you from the inside out. You were never meant to walk this journey alone. I encourage you to reach out and allow me to walk alongside you as we gently uncover and heal the roots contributing to your stress and health struggles. I am very thankful I did, and I trust you will be too!

Breaking the chains and freeing myself from my triggers has been worth every tear I shed. I had to face the beast within so I could release all the deep-seated pain I harbored. It was a difficult process to relive the memories and release the emotions I had buried. I am not going to sugarcoat it. The process is rather tough and took time as I repaired my soul, but it is extremely worthwhile. By no means could I have processed my triggers without the help of professionals. With God's guidance and the practitioner's help, I was able to open wounds that needed to heal so God could reveal my true identity. The love and joy this healing has brought forth is unimaginably wonderful and truly the most significant part in my healing thus far. I will forever be grateful to all the professionals for helping me resurrect my worth.

I echo these words: "Thank You, Lord, that Your plans for my life are good, and that You have a future for me that is full of hope. Thank You that You are continuously restoring my life to greater wholeness. I praise You and thank You that You are my Healer, my Deliverer, my Provider, my Redeemer, my Father, and my Comforter."[64]

God used my triggers to draw my attention inward. Each reaction exposed emotions I had buried as part of survival. If your triggers could speak, what hidden stories, wounds, or unmet needs might they be pointing you toward? Which of your reactions might actually be invitations to reclaim parts of your heart that learned to survive instead of thrive? Healing requires more than awareness—it requires feeling, and that means finally facing our emotions.

Please scan the QR code to explore the songs that impacted my soul as worship became my way through.

Chapter Eleven

EMOTIONS

The meaning we give to anything creates emotion in our body, and our emotions create the life we experience.

—Jamie Kern Lima

Emotions. Where do I even begin? Two phrases I heard often and that irritated me were "You need to deal with your emotions," and "Your emotions are affecting the pain in your body." I will admit I thought these comments were as far-fetched as it comes. I did not agree with the statements at all and truly believed there had to be physical damage to explain why I endured so much pain. I could not comprehend that how I felt emotionally would impact my muscles and nerves. It made no sense! I never could have imagined the profound impact my trapped emotions had on my health.

As I started processing my triggers, I discovered I had a lot of trapped emotions from my childhood. As I worked on releasing these emotions and started to process them, the pain would physically move in my body. If I started with pain in my lower back or around my pelvis area, the next day, after processing a traumatic event and my emotions, the pain moved up into my mid-back area.

The discomfort was so severe at times that Dave had to take me to the emergency room. Twice, the paralyzing pain took my breath away. It felt like a knife stabbing through my ribs, and I could hardly move. I needed help getting off a chair, getting out of bed, and dressing myself as I sobbed in excruciating pain. When I arrived at the emergency room, the doctor assessed me and then injected me with an anti-inflammatory painkiller, also giving me some hydromorphone (a potent, semi-synthetic opioid analgesic). They were convinced my muscles were the culprit, but I knew this pain was different.

The medications barely took the edge off. Trying to sleep or rest while in this state became a true challenge, and comfort was not to be found. Two weeks after the first emergency room visit, when I processed another major event and released trapped emotions, the all-too-familiar stabbing pain returned. I tried to take the discomfort away with the pharmaceutical medication, but nothing helped. Hydromorphone did absolutely nothing for me. During this tormented time, I read a quote which provided some comfort: "The pain you feel today is the strength you'll feel tomorrow." Somehow, hoping tomorrow would bring me strength helped me face another day. I knew it was just a matter of time before this, too, would pass.

As I released all the hurt, the sadness, and the feelings of being unloved, I discovered that my nervous system would often be triggered. The pain I felt in my ribs was, in fact, nerve pain, and unfortunately, nothing would alleviate it. I finally recognized a cycle—one day I processed my trapped emotions, and the next I suffered with physical pain. My counsellor told me to pay attention to what situation I was in when the pain started, and especially who I was with. She said there could be a link to the emotional state I felt, depending on both those factors.

In pursuit of understanding the emotions I had buried, I once again immersed myself in research, hoping to uncover the truths within my pain. I needed to understand what happened within my body as I released my emotions. Did you know emotions involve a mind-body connection? What we refuse to process emotionally, the body absorbs physically. Unresolved trauma often manifests as tension, tightness, or lingering discomfort in the body. Anger may harden the jaw, fear may tighten the chest, abandonment may knot the stomach, and control may stiffen the shoulders. Our bodies often reveal what our heart has not yet released. When we learn to recognize these physical signals, we begin addressing the roots instead of merely the symptoms.

Here are a few examples of emotions manifesting with physical sensations:

- A sense that you've lost control can lead to headaches.

- Feelings of hurt or sadness can be associated with chest pain or discomfort.

- Fear or anxiety can cause stomach discomfort or butterflies.

- Responsibilities and burdens can manifest as tension in the neck and shoulders.

- Anger or frustration can be stored in the lower back.[65]

As I processed the information before me, the connection became undeniable—my emotional wounds were expressing themselves through physical pain. The parts of my body that were affected the most are where anger, fear, sadness, anxiety, depression, and shame reside. Even though I had structural damage to my spine with a bulging disc, disc protrusions, swelling, nerve injury, and muscle injury, the trapped emotions contributed to exacerbating the pain in my body. Processing emotions provided another step in my physical healing journey.

While processing my trapped emotions, I also started using AO Scan technology by Solex.

> AO Scan technology is a unique educational wellness tool that provides users with non-invasive frequency-based feedback. It interacts with the body using subtle bio-frequencies and electromagnetic signals to help users increase awareness of their energetic patterns. By recognizing areas where energetic balance may be supported, individuals can make informed lifestyle and wellness decisions that align with their personal goals for harmony and self-awareness.[66]

AO Scan offers several different features; however, the one I use the most is the inner voice.

The inner voice is a wellness feature that uses vocal tone analysis and personalized auto feedback to support emotional awareness and energetic balance. The process captures a brief voice recording and analyzes 12 tonal frequencies across the chromatic musical scale. The inner voice report highlights frequency variations that may reflect your current emotional expression, providing four supportive audio tones designed to promote a calming and harmonizing experience. Countless users find value in listening to these tones several times a day . . . as part of their wellness or mindfulness routine. Optional color recommendations are also included to support a multisensory experience through visual engagement.[67]

Every morning, through my AO Scan, I was given four emotional tones to listen to, each one guiding me to deeper healing. Often, I would wear the recommended colored glasses while listening to the supportive audio tones in an effort to calm my emotions and balance my energy. The picture labeled "Sadness vs Inner Peace" is an example of the type of report that was emailed to me, offering further insight into each tone and indicating which color of lens I needed to wear. The one I chose to share is one that appeared most frequently during this phase of my healing.

SADNESS vs INNER PEACE

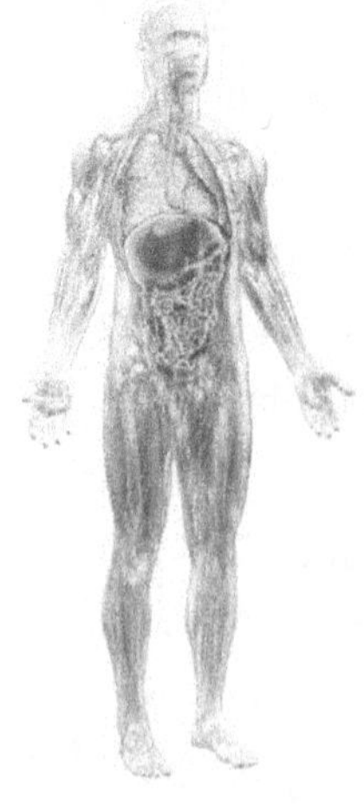

Corresponding Note: D

Positive Emotions

- Inner peace
- Being self accepting and having inner harmony
- Absence of constantly worrying
- No pressuring thoughts associated with the past

Negative Emotions

- Sadness
- May consciously or subconsciously focus on the past to 'make sense' or 'solve' negative experiences and emotions
- May have decreased appetite and energy, or tendency to the opposite, overindulgence
- May negatively impact rational thinking and left brain logical ability
- Often triggered by trauma such as abuse, disappointments, or feelings of failure
- Lifestyle choices may contribute to the issue

Supportive Note: G#

Supportive Color: Blue

Blue Supports: Trust, Loyalty, Wisdom, Self-confidence, Intelligence, Faith, and Truth

EMOTIONS
- Abuse
- Sadness
- Disappointment

VITALS
- Vitamin C
- CoEnzyme Q10
- B3, Nicotinamide

POTENTIAL CAUSES
- Viruses: Adenovirus
- Viruses: Rubella virus
- Parasites: Taenia Saginata

IMBALANCES AND SUGGESTIONS
- Liver: Take pre meal enzymes, Consider a liver Detox Program, Consider Chiropractic Adjustments
- Digestion: Increase Trace Minerals, Take Premeal Digestive Enzymes, Consider Chiropractic Adjustment
- Large Intestine: Improve digestion, Take Pre and Probiotics, Eliminate food sensitivities

Reports generated using AO Scan Technology by Copyright for SOLEX

I will admit, I did not understand the toll unprocessed emotions would take on my health. Over the years, as I continued to stuff emotions, it hindered my health greatly. Chronic stress has done the most damage, both physically and emotionally. The stress rooted in my trapped emotions created one of the greatest hurdles during my healing journey.

Most of us will run away from dealing with our emotions and into whatever we find comfort in. Often, these comforts are undiagnosed addictions. It's easier to get a dopamine hit and numb our feelings than deal with what truly hurts us. I cannot count the number of times I've done this in my life. When overwhelmed and in a state of stress, I would try to numb how I felt with red wine. When I became emotional, I would gravitate toward sugary foods and so-called "comfort food" to feel better, even if only for a few minutes. Anything to take the edge off.

Why did I allow this to happen? Well, that, my friend, is the million-dollar question I had to ask myself. I had to reveal the real hang-up as to why I did not deal with my emotions. It meant I had to learn to communicate my feelings, and, as I mentioned previously, this is a skill I was not taught. Unfortunately, it has become one of my greatest challenges.

It's easier to run away and hide, but we have to face reality, look in a mirror, and deal with things we do not want to deal with. We have to take ownership, seek help, admit that we are broken, apologize, and the list goes on and on. I encourage you to ask the tough question: What is your reason for not processing your emotions? If you truly ponder that question, you will receive information and know exactly where you could start to heal. "I don't have time" is not a valid answer because we make time for the important things in our lives. I knew that if I wanted to get off the merry-go-round I was on, I had to alter my actions.

During this phase of my journey, I watched a powerful sermon series called Alive and Free by Red Rocks Church. Doug Wekenman's sermon stopped me in my tracks; it is called "What's Your Drug of Choice?"[68] What a powerful and eye-opening sermon! This sermon left me pondering my life, and I encourage you to watch it.

After releasing all my trapped emotions and triggers through therapy sessions, I still suffered from nerve pain in my left leg. The pain even transitioned into the bottom of my left foot—the same feeling I had in the right foot for sixteen months when mobility was stripped from me. Baffled and at my wits' end, I could not understand why the pain had started in the bottom of my left foot. I thought I had done everything God asked of me, yet the nerve pain persisted.

At my next physiotherapy appointment, the physiotherapist, too, was stumped as to why the nerve pain was not letting up. He asked me if I was ready to pursue something life-altering. I looked at him and replied that I already had, asking what he was thinking. He said, "The one thing we have not been able to tackle well is your weight." I know he did not say this comment lightly; however, he knows I appreciate the facts. I constantly say, "Give it to me straight." He encouraged me to look up Bright Line Eating and explained it's a drastic lifestyle change. Well, he was not kidding!

In a nutshell, the lifestyle change meant no sugar of any kind except fruit, no flour of any kind, no alcohol, weighing out my allowed quantities and portions for each meal, writing down my food the night before, eating only three times a day, and journaling—all for a lifetime! Well, when I heard the words "for a lifetime," it was as if something died inside me. I gave up! With tears in my eyes, I agreed I would look into this eating plan; however, I left his office feeling defeated.

I know weight loss is not rocket science. I realize extra weight on my joints is not favorable, but it's not like I have not tried to lose weight; this is something I've struggled with my entire life. I can live off salads and the weight will not move; if it does, it is at a snail's pace. Needless to say, the rest of the day I felt depressed, and the river of sorrow kept flowing. I no longer had hope of healing the nerve pain. The news left me devastated and undoubtedly in mourning. I have chosen to share a few of my journal entries from this stage of my journey.

April 29, 2025

Deuteronomy 31:8 (NIV): "The LORD himself goes before you and will be with you; he will never leave you nor forsake you. Do not be afraid; do not be discouraged."

I cried a lot today and was quite down. I feel depressed. I am angry, sad, and frustrated that I have to go through this. I never asked to struggle with weight issues. Why does this have to be my reality? Susan Thompson from Bright Line Eating compared the brain scan of an obese person to that of a drug addict, and the scan appeared the same. Talk about an eye opener! Bright Line Eating makes sense, and I know I can do anything I put my mind to; however, I am grieving the loss of tasty food and freedom. I feel as if everything I enjoy, I have to give up, and it makes me very sad. Lord, I need your help. I need your wisdom, peace, and love to carry me through the stronghold that food has on my mind and body. I pray that you will help me and carry me through, God. Maybe I need to commit to thirty days and go from there, one day at a time. I pray I can see things through your eyes, Lord, in Jesus name I pray, amen.

April 30, 2025

Philippians 2:13 (NLT): "For God is working in you, giving you the desire and the power to do what pleases him."

I've been learning a lot about Bright Line Eating. The dos, the do nots, and I have decided I'm starting tomorrow. What do I have to lose? My left foot is notably sore today. I could not bear weight at all and had to use crutches to walk. I'm just so emotional and sad that this is where I am after everything I have worked through the past few years. I'm tired of struggling all the time. It seems I can not catch a break, yet I know there is a plan. I'm just so sad and tired. Tired of the pain, tired of the trials, tired of the valley. I pray, God, that You will help me. That You will restore me and carry me through these dark days. That You will sustain me and give me strength. I feel lost, I feel weak, and I feel hopeless to rid the nerve pain. I pray that Your will prevails and that You will carry me through, amen.

May 1, 2025

Philippians 4:13 (NLT): "For I can do everything through Christ, who gives me strength."

I woke up early with lots of pain in my left foot. It is really swollen and sore today. I accomplished the Day One challenge and meditation for Bright Line Eating. It was a bit emotional thinking of how I got here. All my weight is back, all the pain, the emotions of shame and failure. Why me, God? I cried for the last time, feeling this way. We will conquer this! I know You are helping me. I will treat my body as the temple of Christ and nourish it with whole, healthy foods. I'm taking this seriously. I want to be free, happy, healthy, and living a vibrant life. I want to have no pain, no restrictions, and live life to its fullest. I know I will conquer this mountain because, God, You are walking with me. I am made in the image of God, and my goal is to look like the image He gave me in my secret place: slender, healthy, whole, happy, vibrant, glowing, and changing lives. God brought me this far, and He will carry me to the end. I will be my true, authentic self. My eyes are fixed on You, Lord. I pray that You will reveal to me what I need to pursue and how I can keep my mind strong. I pray for healing in my foot, my whole body, and I pray I can see things through Your eyes and that I won't grow weary. I pray that You will give me the strength I need to persist and persevere. That You will speak to me through this phase of my healing. I thank You for where I live, God, and I thank You for all You have done and provided me. Help me to love myself, in Jesus name I pray, amen.

As I started the boot camp for Bright Line Eating, I listened to a mastermind class by Susan Peirce Thompson as well. While listening, immediately, certain things I heard resonated with me. Intrigued once again, I knew I was exactly where I was meant to be. God had a purpose in this storm, and before long, I found myself ordering the book *Bright*

Line Eating: The Science of Living Happy, Thin, and Free by Susan Peirce Thompson.[69]

While reading in *Bright Line Eating* (BLE), a switch flipped, and I realized I needed to heal my brain from the damage food had done over the years. I had an addiction, and it was called emotional eating. The further I read in BLE, the more I started connecting the dots, and the reason I struggled became illuminated. I felt comforted when I came across the following phrase: "Understand that you are not 'weak-willed.' You are a human being with a human brain. Weakness has nothing to do with it, and programs that rely on your willpower, in the long term, are dooming you to failure."[70]

All these years, I'd needed a lot of willpower to stick with some of the strict eating plans I'd incorporated. This was turning out to be quite interesting. Internally, I felt this was the answer I'd been searching for all these years. As I kept reading, I was fascinated to learn that even though leptin is present in the blood, the brain does not "see" it. This is due to insulin blocking leptin's ability to communicate with the brain.

One of the most eye-opening lessons for me was learning about downregulation. It's the brain's way of adapting to overstimulation—by thinning out dopamine receptors when they're constantly flooded. Dopamine feels good. Sugar tastes good, and over the past few decades, Western society's sugar consumption has exploded. The problem is, the brain was never designed to handle that level of constant stimulation.

That realization flabbergasted me. Without knowing it, I had dulled my brain's ability to respond to pleasure. And sugar is not the only culprit. Our modern lives are filled with dopamine overload—endless coffee, cigarettes, alcohol, pornography, and drugs like cocaine or amphetamines all contribute. But the truth is, even something as common as excessive sugar and refined flour can have the same effect. I invite you to look at sugar and flour through a different lens—not just as food but as substances that can quietly hijack the brain. In many ways, they function more like drugs than nourishment.

I could not believe what I read. Woah! This was huge! Sugar and flour were to be considered drugs? I paused in disbelief. I'm sure we've all heard the saying that sugar is ten times more addictive than cocaine; however, I felt Susan was onto something greater. While thinking back over the last year and my struggles with mental health, specifically depression and PTSD, I knew food was a contributing factor. I remember my counsellor and physiotherapist encouraging me to eat healthy and to get moving, saying that these were both contributing factors to calming my nervous system and would help with my mental state. The more I sat around self-sabotaging with comfort food, the longer it seemed I struggled with PTSD and depression.

Susan continues to share:

> If, as you read this, you feel bleak and desperate at the thought of going without sugar and flour, I just want to point out that *that*, right there, is dopamine downregulation talking. It's amazing how powerful the feeling can be—we think that, if these foods aren't in our life, then there is nothing good to live for. I know what the feeling of bleakness is like. You'll get through it, I promise. Dopamine receptors do regenerate. You will be fine. You'll be *better* than fine, because soon enough you'll be well on

your way to your goal weight, much happier, much more confident, and free from the damage these substances are inflicting on your brain.[71]

It felt as if Susan had hand crafted that message directly for me. How on earth did she know this was exactly what I experienced in the days leading up to starting Bright Line Eating? In my soul, I sensed this was another sign from God. Healing my brain from the damage flour and sugar had done was my next hurdle. I had to renew my mind as Ephesians 4:22–24 (NIV) declares,

You were taught, with regard to your former way of life, to put off your old self, which is being corrupted by its deceitful desires; to be made new in the attitude of your minds; and to put on the new self, created to be like God in true righteousness and holiness.

I remember thinking back to the Bible and reflecting on what people ate. I felt that Susan was bang on. There was no such thing as sugar in everything they consumed back then. I don't know if you've looked at the ingredients on the products you buy at the supermarket, but I challenge you to read the labels. I am certain you will identify hidden sugar in nearly everything, including spices. It makes sense that our brains are not designed to handle the amounts of sugar we are consuming.

What I discovered next really drove the point home. "Emotions are also very powerful cues. Whether due to boredom, anger, celebratory joy, fear, insecurity, grief, loneliness, frustration, happiness, or sadness, emotional eating is as common today as mindless eating. We even call it 'comfort food,' for goodness' sake!"[72]

> Negative emotions are a cue to eat. . . . If those connections between uncomfortable emotions and hitting that dopamine release valve are hardwired in childhood, over time, emotions become the cues that predict food rewards. When a child is crying a parent does not say, "Would you like some broccoli?" It's usually a cookie, a cracker, or another sugar-or flour-based treat that's offered.[73]

Without realizing it, my life had become filled with constant cues to eat—subtle, powerful, and difficult to escape. But there was a path forward, one intentionally designed to bring freedom where there had been bondage. For healing to take place, my body needed rest. My insulin and dopamine systems had to be given space to recalibrate and return to the balance God designed.

It was evident—just as I had to heal and create new neural pathways in my brain with the Subconscious Mind course, God wanted me to heal my brain from the damage flour and sugar had done as well. I am to heal every part of my brain and subconscious mind.

One of the biggest mistakes made in society today is that we view addiction as merely drugs and alcohol. May I ask why we do not view food, workaholism, cigarettes, caffeine, shopping, sex, fasting, excessive exercise, and gambling as addictions as well? I have continually heard judgement placed on homeless individuals because of their choices. But

I encourage you to examine your own life. If we really reflect on all those forces, they may have done as much damage to our body, mind, and family as drugs and alcohol.

I cannot tell you how many times I ate alone as my husband chose to work. Work is a struggle for him, just as food has been a struggle for me, but did I ever think to tell him to go to AA for workaholics? I can assure you no one has ever encouraged me to go to AA for emotional eating. Why do we pick and choose what addiction is worthy of seeking help? Why do we sense it's okay to be a workaholic or an emotional eater, but if we are an alcoholic or a drug addict, then we need to seek help? This is a very slippery slope, and we need to wake up and be honest with ourselves. I assure you, every one of those addictions causes damage in our lives and to our families.

I strongly encourage you to observe your own family, as I have, and note what the cost of these addictions has been in your life. Trust me, we can appear to have a perfect family and a blessed life outwardly, but I guarantee you there are skeletons in the closet, skeletons of addiction. Well, news flash! Skeletons are silent killers. I encourage you to dig deep and look at which addiction, if any, rings true for you. Trust me, if you don't, destruction will be inevitable; it's merely a matter of time. Healing can awaken us to the dysfunction we once called normal. To truly heal our emotions, we need to identify the root of all our addictions, and we have to fully process them so we can be free once and for all.

After trudging through my trauma and processing my emotional roots, I started reflecting on everything I had encountered. I understood more than ever the impact my childhood had on my life. Being raised in a critical environment led to the addiction of emotional eating at a young age. I understand now that I learned to silence my feelings, believing I could not talk about them because they were not accepted in my home. Regrettably, this was the start of how my trapped emotions came to be. What we experienced in our childhood is what we apply. Everywhere I looked growing up, deep pain and hurts were swept under the rug as if they did not happen. Often I heard, "Place a smile on your face"—a warning not to embarrass our family.

The damage this has done to me, as well as to a great number in our society, is one of the biggest problems Christians face today. Too many of us innocent children were scarred by our families. The emotional and physical abuse I endured while being asked to sit in church on a Sunday morning as if nothing had happened behind closed doors was brutal. I was not taught to have a personal relationship with Jesus. Frankly, I was not taught most of what I know today regarding my faith and how we are to live in response to Christ's love.

As I grew wiser, I found myself carrying a quiet resentment toward the community and church that had shaped my childhood. I witnessed so much destruction and hypocrisy; it was mind-boggling to me how people could call themselves Christians. I could not understand how they did not know better, how they thought this kind of behavior was acceptable. I am not trying to pass judgement on anyone, as that is not my position. However, the Bible is clear, and the answers are not far away if Christians spend time in God's Word.

For instance, Mark 8:34–38 (NLT) states:

> *Then, calling the crowd to join his disciples, he said, "If any of you wants to be my follower, you must give up your own way, take up your cross, and follow me. If you try to hang on*

> *to your life, you will lose it. But if you give up your life for my sake and for the sake of the Good News, you will save it. And what do you benefit if you gain the whole world but lose your own soul? Is anything worth more than your soul? If anyone is ashamed of me and my message in these adulterous and sinful days, the Son of Man will be ashamed of that person when he returns in the glory of his Father with the holy angels."*

1 John 1:5–9 (NLT) declares:

> *This is the message we heard from Jesus and now declare to you: God is light, and there is no darkness in him at all. So we are lying if we say we have fellowship with God but go on living in spiritual darkness; we are not practicing the truth. But if we are living in the light, as God is in the light, then we have fellowship with each other, and the blood of Jesus, his Son, cleanses us from all sin. If we claim we have no sin, we are only fooling ourselves and not living in the truth. But if we confess our sins to him, he is faithful and just to forgive us our sins and to cleanse us from all wickedness.*

Too many people feel they cannot step through the doors of a church. Perhaps because they fear judgement will be passed, maybe they feel they don't have it all together, or they have been hurt by the church. But I am living proof we will never have it all together. I am a work in progress, just as we all will be until the day we meet Jesus. Paul reminds us of this in Philippians 1:6 (NLT),

And I am certain that God, who began the good work within you, will continue his work until it is finally finished on the day when Christ Jesus returns.

I would like to remind you that the church is not the building we meet in but rather the faithful people with whom we surround ourselves. The church is a hospital for the sick. Every one of us is human; we will unfailingly make mistakes; we just need to seek to be Christ-like, respond in obedience, repent, and be willing to try again. We have to be willing to pick up our cross daily. The most impactful sermons I have ever heard are from pastors who are authentic and not afraid to show their brokenness. Those are the ones with whom I can resonate. I want to see the heart of a leader who struggles just as I do. After all, we are the broken that God has transformed for His honor and glory.

I strongly encourage all Christians to lend a hand and help pick people up out of the pit of despair they may be in. Don't stand over them with a "holier than thou" attitude, passing judgement, unless you remain sinless. Jesus confronts this behavior in John 8:7–11 (NIV),

When they kept on questioning him, he straightened up and said to them, "Let any one of you who is without sin be the first to throw a stone at her." Again he stooped down and wrote on the ground. At this, those who heard began to go away one at a time, the older ones first, until only Jesus was left, with the woman still standing there. Jesus straightened up and asked her, "Woman, where are they? Has no one condemned you?" "No one, sir," she said. "Then neither do I

> *condemn you," Jesus declared. "Go now and leave your life*
> *of sin."*

Our goal needs to be living as a testament to what it means to have a personal relationship with Christ, learning to view every situation through His eyes, not our own. When I am able to implement this practice, my heart is filled with love and compassion for others. Through this practice, I am able to mend the damage within myself. I navigate this with a true north compass, consistently gravitating toward God, seeking His wisdom and guidance. We need to remind ourselves that the best sermons are lived, not preached.

As I shifted my focus, I started being grateful for the growth I had accomplished. I have come to learn and accept progress over perfection. I'm still not great at giving myself credit for the progress I've made. The chatter in my mind keeps telling me I am not healed enough; I am not working hard enough; I should be fixed already. Unlearning this critical spirit was a hard feat. Without God's guidance and implementing grace and compassion for myself, I would not have been successful, and I most definitely would not be where I am today. I had to fully recognize that all parts of my journey are a lot for one person to face. God provides strength not merely to survive but to remain resilient as He restores and renews us. Most of all, facing our storms and valleys is necessary so we can be set free. There is healing behind every storm; we just have to weather the storm.

A tool I implemented to help heal my emotions was a vision board. Every January, my daughter and I carve out time to sit together and bring our ideas to life. I begin by cutting out images and phrases that speak to me, not knowing why they resonate. Yet, as I arrange them on my poster board, a story for the year quietly unfolds. I may not understand its full meaning at that moment, but as time passes, each phrase and image holds a purpose for my year.

I am sharing a past vision board and encourage you to consider making one of your own. It is a powerful and creative tool that I often revisit throughout the year and especially read whenever doubt or overwhelm creeps in. It's a gentle reminder to stay grounded and focused on the path ahead.

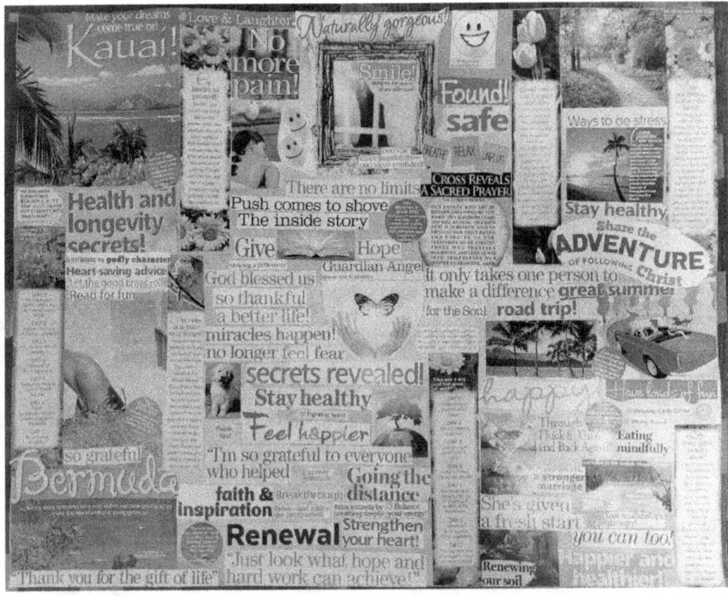

If I could go back in time, I can assure you I would have addressed my trapped emotions immediately, before they had a chance to take root. One of the biggest regrets I have is that I did not know how greatly my emotions would hinder my health as I grew older. The root of emotions was deeply embedded in every root I have shared so far. I would not have struggled so much in life with anger, obedience, forgiveness, control, abandonment, rest, worth, boundaries, fear, and triggers if I had processed my trapped emotions. My prayer is that you, too, will tackle your trapped emotions so that you can be set free and come out on the other side healthier. May my pain and journey help you dig deep and take action in your own life.

Remember, where you look and what you think is where you will end up. Believe in yourself! Believe in your worth! When you can see it, you will start to believe it.

My root of emotions taught me that each feeling surfaced as a messenger, revealing wounds that needed attention and truth that could no longer be ignored. But awareness brought a sobering realization—healing does not happen instantly. That truth led me to the next root: patience.

Please scan the QR code to hear the songs that lifted my spirit and reminded me that God's promises never fail.

PART FOUR: RISE

Living authentically means rising from the ashes
and embracing who we are in Christ.

—Constance André

Chapter Twelve
PATIENCE

When I peeled back the layers I found a beautiful resilience inside.
This is how I know I'll always thrive.

—Lori Schaefer

Now, let's get real! Who can honestly say they have patience? I think we can all muster patience for a little while, maybe a few minutes, maybe through a few failed attempts, but I am pretty certain that eventually, we *all* will become frustrated and our patience will wear thin.

Patience is more than just waiting—it is trusting in God's timing and wisdom, even through the storms and uncertainty we face. It is an active form of surrender and reliance on God, which helps us navigate the valleys without losing hope. As a fruit of the Spirit, patience is not something we manufacture on our own; it is cultivated as we abide in God and allow Him to shape our hearts.

Patience is also about managing our inner being. It is the ability to "accept the things we cannot change" and allows us to feel emotions without letting them dictate our actions. Patience creates space for circumstances to unfold naturally and helps us slow down, allowing us to truly listen, understand, and respond with intention rather than react out of frustration.

To say I was impatient through the turbulent storms I faced would be an understatement. Being patient while enduring long suffering, amongst a huge uprooting, is certainly not my forte. I would have preferred not to have suffered the amount that I have. Who am I kidding? I would have done *anything* I could to rid myself of the nerve pain I had to endure. I must admit, although I felt as though I was pushed further into the flames along my journey, I have come to recognize that sometimes the pain has to intensify before it can be relieved.

Too many times while waiting for healing, worry, fear, and doubt creep into our thoughts. We have things to do, places to go, and people to see. We have a reputation to uphold and work to be done. We do not have time to sit around and wait for healing. But, because of my lack of patience during this phase, sometimes I unravelled—especially when I was not healed according to my plan or my expectations. Waiting for physical healing is truly one of the hardest challenges I have had to face through my journey, and, unfortunately, it still plagues me. I have learned, though, that we have to shift our mindset and the lens through which we look. We have to *trust* God's plan and "die" to ourselves. When negativity creeps in, we have to remember to use our coping strategy tools. If I had not done so, I certainly would not be where I am today.

Sometimes, we like to blame every hardship or suffering we face on God instead of trusting His will for our lives. What drives us to act this way? I have witnessed numerous people who don't worship God, or even believe he exists, blame Him for sickness or death. Why does everyone know where to find God to blame Him but refuse to believe in His truth or have faith in Him? I have blamed God for more than my share of circumstances; trust me, I am not innocent. I did so because I needed to hold someone accountable when there was no one else I could blame. My human nature, out of desperation, craved accountability—a need I have had to learn to release and surrender to God. Who or what have you been holding responsible for your pain—and are you willing to surrender that burden to the One who can actually heal it?

I know that God wants my undivided attention. What better way to start than to teach me patience in the midst of suffering? Smart move on God's part, I must say. I strongly believe that's why setbacks keep happening to me. God chose to shake up my life to keep my attention. He knew to obtain my undivided attention, He needed to take away the one thing I could not control: my health. Even though it frustrated me more times than I can count during my healing, God shook up my life so He could transform my perspective. During this transformation, I became a follower of Jesus, not just a believer in Jesus. This transformation needed to happen because I am called to live out His plan for my life, not my plan for my life. Cara Whitney describes this process perfectly:

> God shakes up our lives to get our attention when we start
> trusting that false sense of happiness the world
> provides. . . . God is a loving father. He shakes the bucket
> to protect his children, not to upset, hurt, or punish them.

> He wants to lead us back to the safety of the specific path
> He has for each of us.[74]

God used the following scripture to profoundly shape my healing journey. This passage anchored my understanding of patience and became a cornerstone in my transformation. James 1:2–8 (NLT) states:

> *Dear brothers and sisters, when troubles of any kind come your way, consider it an opportunity for great joy. For you know that when your faith is tested, your endurance has a chance to grow. So let it grow, for when your endurance is fully developed, you will be perfect and complete, needing nothing. If you need wisdom, ask our generous God, and he will give it to you. He will not rebuke you for asking. But when you ask him, be sure that your faith is in God alone. Do not waver, for a person with divided loyalty is as unsettled as a wave of the sea that is blown and tossed by the wind. Such people should not expect to receive anything from the Lord. Their loyalty is divided between God and the world, and they are unstable in everything they do.*

I truly believe that to experience the joyfulness and the great expectancy of healing, my suffering needed to be drawn out. Let's just say, my "challenger" spirit had a hard time surrendering. In my entire life, I have not been recognized as the most patient person, and this is why I believe God asked me to work on this root last. I had to confront and heal all the other roots within me before I could create space for patience to grow. I also believe that if my health issues had not been drawn out, I might have taken my healing for granted and therefore not been obedient to what God asked of me. When I had no control over the pain I endured, I was forced to look to my true healer, God. He had my undivided attention even though He got the brunt of my fury. God has a plan for me just as He does for you, and I needed to *trust* and endure the waiting.

As I was reading *Waymaker*, Ann Voskamp reminded me that

> Waiting is a letting go to let something grow. The waiting need not destroy the soul but *grow* the soul. Waiting is a kind of expecting—expecting to have the capacity for hope and pain and love and life to expand. . . . The longer we wait, the larger we become, and the more joyful our expectancy.[75]

Undoubtedly, my patience needed to grow for God's work to be completed in me. When it became clear I had to accept His plan instead of insisting on my own, waiting became easier, and I could feel my patience beginning to take hold.

God also reminded me that I needed to be patient with others and myself, just as Ephesians 4:2 (NLT) declares: "Always be humble and gentle. Be patient with each other, making allowance for each other's faults because of your love."

Another unexpected catalyst for growing my patience came through studying personality and leadership styles. In that exploration, God revealed wisdom I hadn't previously seen.

> All personalities reflect God in their own way. No one has
> a 360° view of life or leadership. *We need each other.* This
> is not weakness; this is how the Body of Christ is intended
> to function. We each bring needed strengths to the table.
> Together, we more fully reflect the image and the heart
> of God. . . . Cooperation and communication are key.
> Gaining a basic understanding of how our teammates
> think, interact, and how they approach leadership sets us
> up for success to work well together. [76]

Personality style tests have helped me immensely. I recognized that I needed to be open to seeing other people for who Christ made them to be, not who I expected them to be. It is a humbling experience to look at my negative personality traits. A turning point, if you will. With the help of these tests, I have been able to work on my weaknesses and dial back my strengths. I recognized that I had to place myself in the other person's shoes so that I could see the bigger picture. Because of this knowledge, I have been able to pinpoint why I have struggled with certain relationships. It could be something as silly as expecting something from someone when they are physically incapable because of their personality type. Trust me, you will want to look into these tests if you have not done so. You will see relationships differently if you pursue this, and your patience for others and yourself will start to grow. The link is in the endnotes.[77]

During September 2025, I had the privilege of attending a Zach Williams concert—unaware that another setback was quietly approaching. While walking through the airport, I heard a loud pop, and my left hamstring promptly went on holiday—abandoning me to waves of pain as I fought to keep moving. Though I have come leaps and bounds and see the positive changes in my healing, I indisputably know God is not done with me yet. Everything I endure carries purpose—this much I know with absolute certainty. The following day brought yet another setback. While asleep in my bed, my left calf muscle violently spasmed, leaving my entire left leg barely functional. I will openly acknowledge how deeply discouraged this made me. I had been savoring my freedom from pain, only to realize God clearly had other plans.

Why did I need to endure more suffering? The answer felt simple, though not easy: to grow my character and strengthen my faith. I have come to view these setbacks as tests—opportunities to reveal whether I will practice patience and turn my heart toward Him in the middle of my struggle. As I stood in front of my friends and family, tears streamed down my cheeks as the pain intensified. I kept praying for relief and healing, clinging to the hope that God was still near. Patience while suffering does not come quickly—and perhaps it never fully will. We are not designed to carry burdens alone. With His help, I will continue to persevere.

Pain and suffering are frequently the means by which we become motivated to finally surrender to God and to seek the cure of Christ. Not all of us learn and benefit from suffering; that's where free will comes in.[78]

Every time I am faced with a challenge, I have to remind myself to surrender my will and look to God for the silver lining. One would think I would have this down to a science by now, but I definitely do not. It may take me a few minutes, a few hours, or even days before I realize the path I should take; however, I do see a lot of growth in my perspective when enduring suffering. I recognize now that when faced with struggles, I need to seek God first. I no longer respond with the anger that once consumed me. I don't enter the party of self-pity, and I can now say with gratitude that, with God, I have finally conquered this remarkable obstacle. When I returned home from the concert, I still struggled to walk, but my husband commented, "You're handling this setback really well compared to in the past." I was content to hear those words because it meant my internal change was now reflected on the outside.

Our life is the biggest testimony of our faith that we can live. If our heart is truly transformed and present with God, our life and actions will be as well. I am not saying I am perfect because I am far from perfect; however, I try my hardest to be a living example of my faith at all times.

As I lingered with God in a devotional one day, the message of His grace finally broke through in a way that reshaped my understanding.

> How wonderful that God's Spirit in us writes a story of grace and redemption! For as meaningful as written words can be, it is our lives that are the best witness to the truth of the gospel, for they speak volumes through our compassion, service, gratitude, and joy. Through our words and actions, the Lord spreads His life-giving love.[79]

While reading *Rescue Story* by Zach Williams, God reminded me of what He is capable of. Even when I don't see Him, He is working. I wholeheartedly agree with Zach that "The only thing rearview mirrors are good for [is] looking back to be grateful."[80] I will forever be grateful for the restoration He has provided. Putting aside my own healing, thoughts, and feelings, He powerfully spoke to me through Zach's words, affirming His plan for my life.

When you hand your mess of a life over to God like I did, He can take all the broken pieces and put together something you never dreamed possible. The interesting thing is that He won't do that unless you give it *all* to Him. Yet once you begin to see and experience God pulling everything together, life will start to make sense, often for the first time. You begin to understand why He has allowed certain things in your life and what He can do. . . .God can use any of us best when we remain in the mysterious balance of living out our healing, while remembering our brokenness.[81]

Powerful emotions overwhelmed me as everything Zach said resonated in every inch of my body. He took the words right out of my mouth! I, too, choose to remember where I came from and how God used every moment to shape who I am today. God is powerful! He transformed and healed what I did not think was possible. Often, I reflect and ask myself why God chose me. But I know in my soul that He uses the broken to do His will. Just look at how He used Paul in the Bible. God has a greater plan than I can even comprehend, and I *trust* His will for my life no matter what obstacles I need to face. To solidify this new mindset, I share a final journal entry.

July 3, 2025

I am fully trusting God to help navigate my path and open the doors for me. I pray that my story will powerfully help others heal by encouraging them through the storms. I feel called to coach, speak at events, and pursue this uncharted territory. As I sit here in the early morning listening to all the different sounds of the wind chime, birds, wind, and leaves fluttering, I am so grateful that this is my life. So grateful I made it, and God gave me the strength. I am thankful for the beauty that surrounds me and the blessings my life truly holds. I love my sunny morning coffee on the deck. It fills my soul and mind with such peace, joy, and contentment. Lord, I thank You for Your beautiful creation. I thank You for healing me, for guiding me, and for providing for me. I trust Your will and plan for my life, my book, my health, and my finances. I trust Your timing and what I am supposed to learn through the process. In Jesus Name I pray, amen.

Jesus is the only one who can truly help us succeed in this life, and He helps us conquer the impossible, because in Him, nothing is impossible. "If all we're going to do is look at the mountain ahead of us instead of who created the mountain, we will always feel overwhelmed."[82]

We all need deliverance at one time or another. That's because no matter how spiritual we are, we're still made of flesh. And no matter how perfectly we live, we still have an enemy who is trying to erect strongholds of evil in our lives. God wants us free from everything that binds, holds, or separates us from Him.[83]

Please scan the QR code to hear my heart's anthem, a reflection of the healing God completed within me.

EPILOGUE

As you surrender everything—your fears, your plans, your need for control—you don't lose yourself; you shed what was never truly yours. In letting go, you are beautifully transformed and finally set free.

—Constance André

Everything the Lord revealed in the midst of my healing journey has been truly life-altering. On December 24, 2024, while at our church Christmas Eve service, God spoke the name of this book into my heart. The moment the words landed, I recognized the familiar pull of obedience—quiet, firm, and unmistakable. I did not feel ready, but I felt called. I did not wait for clarity, confidence, or comfort. I simply said yes and began writing the following day.

Along the way, as truth unfolded, a vital lesson appeared: physical healing is deeply connected to our mindset. Our brains are naturally wired to see the negative, and when we experience trauma, that tendency is amplified. I witnessed firsthand the incredible power of my thoughts and how profoundly they affect my entire being. Because of this, I made changing my mindset a top priority. I am actively creating new neural pathways filled with positivity to replace my old, limiting beliefs that silently hindered me. Focusing on gratitude has become a key practice, training me to look for the good in every circumstance—even the less desirable ones.

For my worth to be resurrected, I had to peel back *all* the layers, not just the ones I was willing to peel. These layers are all the roots I have written about in these pages. As I processed these roots, I faced what had happened, felt the depths of the pain it left within me, and *surrendered* it all to God, who alone could bring complete inner restoration. As you have read, I struggled greatly while healing to the core. It was a difficult and painful road as God led me. Healing requires an open mind, courage, resilience, and patience. When I finally relinquished control and allowed God to reign, everything fell into place, and my healing was made complete through Him.

I chose to forgive in the process of freeing myself and let God be the judge and jury. I chose to embrace discomfort and accept change. I now value my true, authentic self and live in the higher frequencies of life.

I have established healthy boundaries and, for the first time in my life, truly see my worth. To support my well-being, I intentionally carve out time for myself—spending quiet moments with God, admiring His creation, praying, nourishing my body with healthy food, exercising, and practicing EFT tapping.

I understood which character traits were rooted in survival programming and needed healing. My perfectionism and need for control topped that list—and I know I am not alone in this battle, as many of us struggle with those same traits. What parts of your personality were shaped by survival—and are you ready to invite healing where control once felt necessary?

I discovered that taking things personally often stemmed from unresolved wounds of the past that needed to be dealt with. Most importantly, I sensed I had to surrender *everything* and turn to my true healer, God. He holds all the answers. The question is whether we will listen and choose to obey.

For a long time, I pursued healing again and again, but I never gave myself permission to truly feel the emotions woven into those painful scars. I never fully surrendered or gave God control over them. Unfortunately, I needed to be forced to deal with the pain I harbored. Pain that I now know changed the course of who I was meant to be.

Did I ever think this day would come? Definitely not. Would I have confronted the pain on my own? No, I do not believe I would have. For nearly thirty-five years of my life, I left roots buried so deep that I didn't dare look back while slowly self-destructing. Yet, through it all, I am extremely grateful that God patiently and gracefully helped me endure seasons of long suffering and hardships. I could not have overcome those roots or experienced true healing without fully trusting His guidance.

Even through the darkest days, God kept providing for me. One provision came as I earned the Hat Trick Award.

The *Hat Trick Award* is a recognition of outstanding achievement, honoring the person who has reached multiple significant milestones in a short period of time. Constance André is a truly deserving recipient, having accomplished not one, but three remarkable feats in just six months. Her success in the Fast Starter Program, the Fast Start Manager, and the Founders Challenge showcases her exceptional dedication, unwavering commitment, and remarkable resilience. These three accomplishments highlight Constance's unwavering commitment, adaptability, and resilience. She consistently delivers outstanding results while maintaining focus and determination in the face of challenges. Her growth mindset and ability to excel across different programs and challenges make her the perfect recipient of the *Hat Trick Award*. Constance's journey serves as an inspiration, showing that with hard work and dedication, anything is possible. Big congratulations to you, Constance.

Needless to say, I stood in awe! I felt deeply honored to receive such an award. Amidst all my struggles, pain, and heartache, I could hardly believe that I made a meaningful impact on those around me. God faithfully provided exactly what my heart needed at every step on my journey.

That same night I received the award, I was also handed a precious gift with the following engraving: "*Difference Maker*, a dedicated individual who can make a big impact even with just a small action or a few words. Someone who makes a difference in the lives of others."

I am extremely thankful. This entire experience magnifies that even in our darkest times and struggles, we do not know who is watching. Our lives, words, and actions can leave a lasting impression on those around us—sometimes in ways we could not imagine.

Throughout the turbulent storms I faced, I am pleased to say I have accomplished post-traumatic growth:

> A positive psychological change experienced by some people after a traumatic event, representing a transformation beyond previous levels of functioning. This growth isn't the absence of distress but a way of making sense of adversity, leading to new understandings of oneself, others, and the world, often resulting in increased personal strength, appreciation for life, new possibilities, stronger relationships, and spiritual change.[84]

With resilience and courage, I faced my fears. I yielded and fully trusted God's plan, even when I could not see it or make sense of it. I endured the discomfort of growth and discovered the beauty of vulnerability as I stepped into my authentic self. I took ownership of my mistakes and chose grace over pride. Through it all, I wouldn't change a single moment because I am finally *free!* I am living the life God always intended for me.

As I reflect on my healing journey, I am finally able to piece together the puzzle of my life with clarity. Each connection reminds me of everything

God provided each step of the way. I take time to reflect so I can remember where I've been, what I endured, and where I am now.

Someone asked me, "What does surrendering feel like in your body?" I didn't answer right away and paused with the question for days. What finally surfaced was tug-of-war—a relentless pulling between release and resistance. The more I listened, the more I grasped the truth beneath it: my inner child was still gripping tightly because she did not feel safe enough to let go. As I reflect now, I wonder what this same question stirs in you. What rises to the surface when you ask yourself how surrendering feels in your body?

For me, feeling safe enough to expose my authentic self became the ultimate hurdle for complete healing to fall into place. True surrender—laying down every human instinct to control, protect, and perform—doesn't happen all at once. It comes in layers. God does not ask for everything at once; He reveals the next step only when we are ready, and when the season is right to receive His direction, as John 16:12 (NLT) declares:

> *There is so much more I want to tell you, but you can't bear it now.*

Storms are inevitable in our lives. But those storms have a way of revealing the condition of our faith. Do we pause long enough to see the significance of our suffering? Or do we fixate on the wrong questions—asking, "Why?" instead of, "What is being formed within us?"

Through this process, I discovered that healing is not about perfection—it is about direction. It is a brave decision to turn and walk in obedience even when the path feels uncertain. And in that obedience, God transformed my doubts into bold declarations of faith that I now live out daily.

Already, through my journey, I have had the privilege of impacting others—whether it is someone I met in distress, offering an encouraging word, or someone I'm praying for. God has given me a heart of compassion and the ability to see beyond surface issues to reach the root of the matter. I can now relate more deeply, and I know that it is God working through me. A scripture that affirms my thoughts is found in 2 Corinthians 1:4–6 (NLT):

He comforts us in all our troubles so that we can comfort others. When they are troubled, we will be able to give them the same comfort God has given us. For the more we suffer for Christ, the more God will shower us with his comfort through Christ. Even when we are weighed down with troubles, it is for your comfort and salvation! For when we ourselves are comforted, we will certainly comfort you. Then you can patiently endure the same things we suffer.

In this season of my life, I am not completely physically healed. There are still moments when my nervous system flares, causing my muscles to tense and my body to react. My nervous system remains sensitive to the world around me, and I must continually use the tools I have learned about to cope and stay grounded.

I find myself seeking God—first to understand others and then to be understood. That, I believe, is the true mark of transformation. Whenever I face discomfort, whether emotional or physical, my first instinct is to look up and seek Him. In doing so, I am filled with a peace that defies explanation.

Communication is a choice—it does not happen by chance. Your body is speaking; will you listen and take the necessary steps to make it whole? Will you face the *impossible,* as I did, and rise into the fullness of your identity as a child of God? I assure you, "With man this is impossible, but with God all things are possible" (Matthew 19:26, NIV).

"God doesn't call the qualified, He qualifies the called."[85]

May my ideas and offerings, my healing journey, and God now support you to make it through your own journey, whatever it may be and wherever you are on it.

You are worthy! The moment you can truly see it, your heart will begin to believe it!

Please scan the QR code to listen to the songs that rose from my altar of worship, each one a reminder of His unfailing faithfulness.

ACKNOWLEDGEMENTS

First and foremost, I thank God for walking with me through every step of this journey. He opened my eyes, strengthened my spirit, and gave me the resilience to seek Him wholeheartedly. Thank you, Lord, for restoring the child of God within me. I will forever be grateful for this once-in-a-lifetime gift.

David, from the bottom of my heart, I want to thank you for not giving up on me. You have stood beside me through the wild adventures God has led me on, and even when you could not see what I saw, your trust did not waver. Thank you for loving me unconditionally during the hardest of times and for supporting me the best you knew how through sickness. Thank you for balancing my lionhearted spirit and keeping me grounded.

My darling Raelyn, thank you for loving me unconditionally through every storm. Thank you for carrying more than any child ever should, for stepping up when I could not, for the laughter that lifted my spirit, and for the hugs that soothed my pain. You are my heart and my greatest motivation. Watching you grow has inspired me to heal deeply so that generational strength—not generational pain—would be passed forward. My deepest prayer is that you will learn from my mistakes and walk boldly on the path God has prepared for you. I am so incredibly proud of you, my precious girl. I love you to infinity and beyond.

Shorty, you are the sister I could only have prayed for, and I love you dearly. Your unwavering support and encouragement over the years have meant more to me than words can fully capture. You always seem to know exactly what I need—whether it's tough love or gentle reassurance. Thank you for never losing faith in my vision or in who I am, even when I struggled to believe in myself. Thank you for helping me see the good when I lost sight of it, for cheering me on wherever God's path has led, and for helping me bring my logo and book design ideas to life. Your gifts and your heart do not go unnoticed. You are a precious gem.

Debbie, thank you so incredibly much for being willing to be the first person to read my memoir. I am deeply grateful for your knowledge, insight, and remarkable editing abilities. God speaks profoundly through you and has guided my story through the gift He's placed within you. We have shared numerous laughs throughout this editing process, and I am truly honored that you were the first person to experience my story. I know God aligned our paths for a reason, and I trust His process as this journey continues to unfold.

I would like to express my gratitude to my friends and family who have supported me along this journey—whether with words of encouragement or a well-timed kick in the pants when I needed it most. The past several years have been some of the toughest I have ever faced, and I am so grateful to have had you in my corner, cheering me on. Your encouragement has meant more to me than you will ever know, and I will hold it dearly in my heart.

I sincerely thank all the professional therapists who have supported me throughout my healing journey. Thank you for being willing to navigate this complex jigsaw puzzle with me and help my body return to what it was meant to be. I am grateful for all the insight and valuable knowledge I have gained over the years. I would not be where I am today without your guidance and care. Each of you contributed in unique ways, whether you realized it at the time or not. Some of the most powerful healings I have experienced have come through these sessions, and I will forever be grateful to each of you for your role in my healing journey.

I would like to thank Elisha Rose for taking the time to guide me as I ventured into the uncharted territory of writing my memoir. Your heartfelt opinions and thoughtful insight have meant more to me than words can express. I am deeply grateful for your continued support and love.

Abigail Young, thank you for making the space to take on the final proofread of my manuscript. You are a truly gifted individual, and I am so grateful for the care and precision you brought to the final adjustments before print. I sincerely appreciate your time and thoughtfulness.

Brenda A. Haire, thank you for your invaluable guidance and unwavering support in helping me bring my book across the finish line. You brought my words to life, and I am incredibly grateful for your remarkable editing abilities. Your creativity and care in fine-tuning my book cover brought my vision to life, creating something I truly love. I believe God aligned our paths, and I am fully trusting His plan for the future and the lives He intends to touch through *Resurrected Worth*. I am proud to be published under A Worthy Press.

MUSIC THAT ANCHORED MY HEALING

Chapter 1—Anger

Micah Tyler. "People Like Us." Single. Fair Trade Services, 2018.

Evan Craft. "Chances." Single. Independent / Evan Craft Music, 2020.

Zach Williams. "Jesus Loves." From the album *Survivor: Live from Harding Prison*. Provident Label Group / Essential Records, 2021.

Chapter 2—Obedience

Jeremy Camp. "Keep Me in the Moment." Single; featured on *The Story's Not Over* (Soundtrack). Stolen Pride Records/Capitol Christian Music Group, 2019.

Casting Crowns, CAIN. "Desert Road." Single on *Healer*. Provident Label Group, 2023.

Bethel Music, Jenn Johnson (feat. Chris Quilala). "Send Me." Track on *Homecoming (Live)*. Bethel Music, 2021.

Chapter 3—Forgiveness

Sidewalk Prophets. "Where Forgiveness Is Found." Track on *These Simple Truths*. Word/Curb Records, 2009.

The Afters. "God Is With Us." Track on *Light Up the Sky*. INO Records, 2010.

Lincoln Brewster. "Made New." Track on *Oxygen*. Integrity Music, 2014.

Chapter 4—Control

Sidewalk Prophets. "There's a Way." Track on *Live Like That*. Word/Curb Records, 2012.

Zach Williams (feat. Dolly Parton). "There Was Jesus." Single. Provident Label Group, 2020.

Zach Williams. "Rescue Story." Track on *Rescue Story*. Provident Label Group, 2018.

Chapter 5—Abandonment

Brandon Ray. "Hold On." Single. 2020.

Jet Trouble. "Heaven Come Down." Single.

Cory Asbury. "Everything Belongs." Track on *To Love a Fool*. Bethel Music, 2020.

Chapter 6—Rest

TobyMac. "Help Is On the Way." Track on *Life After Death*. ForeFront Records, 2021.

Jet Trouble. "I Need You." Track on *An Honest Prayer*. TroubleHasbun Publishing, 2025.

Olivia Lane. "Who God Says You Are." Single. Centricity Music, 2020.

Jeremy Camp. "Wilderness." Track on *When I Speak*. Capitol CMG, 2021.

Chapter 7—Worth

Lauren Daigle. "You Say." Single. Centricity Music/Warner Bros./12Tone, 2018.

Finding Favour. "Old Soul." Single. Gotee Records, 2019.

Casting Crowns. "One Awkward Moment." Single. Beach Street Records, 2021.

Megan Woods. "The Truth." Single. Fair Trade Services, 2024.

Chapter 8—Boundaries

Jet Trouble, Lexi Dean. "God's Hand." Track on *An Honest Prayer*. TroubleHasbun Publishing, 2025.

Pat Barrett. "Every Good Thing." Single. Bowyer & Bow/Sparrow/Capitol CMG, 2023.

Josiah Queen, Brandon Lake. "Can't Steal My Joy." Single. F&L Label Group/Capitol CMG/Josiah Queen Music, 2025.

Chapter 9—Fear

Phil Wickham. "Battle Belongs." Single. Fair Trade Services, 2020.

Jon Reddick. "No Fear." Track on *No Fear*. Gotee Records, 2025.

Jack Cassidy. "Let Go, Let God." Single. Fair Trade Services, 2021.

Josh Baldwin. "I Speak Jesus." Single. Bethel Music, 2024.

Chapter 10—Triggers

Leanna Crawford. "Fragile Heart." Track on *Crazy Beautiful You (Deluxe) EP*. Provident Label Group/Story House Music, 2018.

Jeffrey East. "Because Of Yours." Single. Dreams & Wonder Records, 2024. EastNashville Records, 2019.

Andy Grammer. "Don't Give Up on Me." Track on *Naive*. S-Curve Records, 2019.

Big Daddy Weave, Jason Gray. "Good Grief." Track on *Let It Begin*. Curb Records, 2025.

Chapter 11—Emotions

Evan Craft. "Fight On My Knees." Single. Evan Craft Music/Universal Music Group, 2022.

The Color. "Too Many Times." Track on *No Greater Love*. DREAM Records, 2021.

Katy Nichole, Big Daddy Weave. "God Is in This Story." Single. Centricity Music/Word Entertainment, 2022.

Chapter 12—Patience

Crowder. "Somebody Prayed." Track on *I Know a Ghost*. sixstepsrecords/Sparrow Records/Capitol CMG, 2018.

Leeland. "Better Word." Track on *Better Word*. Integrity Music, 2019.

Ryan Stevenson. "Mosaic." Single. Gotee Records, 2021.

Zach Williams. "Friend in High Places." Track on *Rescue Story*. Provident Label Group/Sony Music Nashville, 2019.

Epilogue

Caleb & John. "Finished." Single. Caleb & John Music under exclusive license to Fair Trade Services, LLC, 2025.

Consumed by Fire, Cochren & Co. "Walk With Jesus." Single. Red Street Records, 2024.

Cross Connection Music. "Shine." Single. Released January 9, 2026, Cross Connection Music Group.

About the Author

Constance André is an entrepreneur, author, and trauma-informed coach whose faith in God fuels her mission to inspire and uplift those who are hurting. As the founder of Valley View Accounting and Resurrected Worth, and an Independent BEMER Distributor, she blends practical wisdom with spiritual insight to guide others toward healing, freedom, and restored purpose.

Constance has also contributed to the anthologies *Dear Beloved Scribe* and *What Should I Do With My Life?* Through compassionate yet courageous guidance, she coaches others to process trauma, confront root wounds, and rediscover their authentic, God-given worth. Her ability to speak truth with both grace and a growth mindset reminds readers that, with faith, perseverance, and dedication, transformation is possible.

As a successful entrepreneur and recipient of the Hat Trick Award, Constance exemplifies dedication, adaptability, and resilience—qualities that empower her to achieve meaningful impact even in the face of adversity.

She is a devoted child of God, wife, and mother who finds joy in cooking, traveling, exploring God's creation, and riding her Harley-Davidson. Music speaks deeply to her soul, offering both solace and strength. Constance resides with her family on a cattle ranch in British Columbia, Canada.

What's Your Next Step?

If this message stirred something in you,
don't let it end here.

Resurrected Worth is more than a book—it's a
journey into healing, identity, and living boldly
in who God says you are.

Continue the journey:
- Take the Course
- Apply for Coaching
- Bring Constance to Your Next Event

Because when one woman's worth is
resurrected, generations are impacted.

ENDNOTES

1. Chip Ingram and Becca Johnson, *Overcoming Emotions That Destroy: Practical Help for Those Angry Feelings That Ruin Relationships* (Grand Rapids: Baker Books, 2009).

2. Ingram and Johnson, *Overcoming Emotions*, 79–80.

3. Ingram and Johnson, *Overcoming Emotions*, 17.

4. Ingram and Johnson, *Overcoming Emotions*, 25.

5. Ingram and Johnson, *Overcoming Emotions*, 52–53.

6. Ingram and Johnson, *Overcoming Emotions*, 85.

7. Ingram and Johnson, *Overcoming Emotions*, 84.

8. Stormie Omartian, *The Power of a Praying Woman* (Eugene, OR: Harvest House Publishers, 2002).

9. Stormie Omartian, *The Power of a Praying Woman 365-Day Desk Calendar* (Nashville: DaySpring, 2018), March 22.

10. Omartian, *The Power of a Praying Woman 365-Day Desk Calendar*, March 10.

11. Ben Woodward, March 5, 2025, BEMER Training, The Entrepreneurial Mindset.

12. Omartian, *The Power of a Praying Woman 365-Day Desk Calendar*, March 21.

13. Omartian, *The Power of a Praying Woman 365-Day Desk Calendar*, March 17.

14. Omartian, *The Power of a Praying Woman 365-Day Desk Calendar*, March 1.

15. Omartian, *The Power of a Praying Woman 365-Day Desk Calendar*, March 7.

16. Omartian, *The Power of a Praying Woman 365-Day Desk Calendar*, February 29.

17. Omartian, *The Power of a Praying Woman 365-Day Desk Calendar*, March 2.

18. Rob Reimer, *Soul Care: Seven Transformational Principles for a Healthy Soul*, 2nd ed. (Franklin, TN: Carpenter's Son Publishing, 2016), 65, 66.

19. Reimer, *Soul Care*, 58–59.

20. Reimer, *Soul Care*, 65–66.

21. Enneagram Institute, "Type Eight: The Challenger," accessed April 15, 2025, https://www.enneagraminstitute.com/type-8.

22. Ann Voskamp, *WayMaker: Finding the Way to the Life You've Always Dreamed Of* (Nashville, TN: Thomas Nelson, 2022).

23. Voskamp, *WayMaker*, 85.

24. Voskamp, *WayMaker*, 85.

25. Brandon Ray, "Hold On," featuring Lauren Weintraub, Denim on Denim Records, 2021, Spotify.

26. TobyMac, "Help Is on the Way (Maybe Midnight)," track on *Life After Death*, ForeFront Records / Capital CMG, 2021.

27. Jamie Kern Lima, *Worthy: How to Believe You Are Enough and Transform Your Life* (Carlsbad, CA: Hay House, 2024), 111.

28. Lima, *Worthy*.

29. Lima, *Worthy*.

30. Lima, *Worthy*, 2, 5.

31. Lima, *Worthy*, 23.

32. Lima, *Worthy*, 127.

33. Take a look at the stunning cathedral on the official website: CatedraldeMallorca.org/en/

34. Lima, *Worthy*, 86.

35. Cuevas del Drach, "History," Cuevas del Drach, Mallorca, accessed October 15, 2025, https://www.cuevasdeldrach.com/en/historia.php.

36. Lima, *Worthy*, 38.

37. Marianne Williamson, *A Return to Love: Reflections on the Principles of "A Course in Miracles"* (New York: HarperCollins, 1992), 52.

38. Lima, *Worthy*, 55–56.

39. Hillsong Worship, "Who You Say I Am," written by Ben Fielding and Reuben Morgan, track 3 on *There Is More*, Hillsong Music, 2018, song.

40. Ziad K. Abdelnour and Wesley A. Whittaker, *Economic Warfare: Secrets of Wealth Creation in the Age of Welfare Politics* (United States: Gildan Media, 2020).

41. Lima, *Worthy*, 92.

42. Kristen Butler, attributed online (Instagram/LinkedIn post), accessed May 18, 2025.

43. Lima, *Worthy*, 159.

44. Lima, *Worthy*, 56–57.

45. Lima, *Worthy*, 65.

46. Lima, *Worthy*, 93.

47. Lima, *Worthy*, 126.

48. Brené Brown. *Rising Strong*. New York: Spiegel & Grau, 2015.

49. Lima, *Worthy*, 162.

50. Lima, *Worthy*, 235.

51. Brian Weiner, *Brian Weiner—Changing the World One Thought at a Time* (February 18, 2022).

52. Lima, *Worthy*, 233.

53. Charity Gayle and Steven Musso, "I Speak Jesus," *Single*, recorded 2022, digital audio, Curb | Word Entertainment.

54. Lima, *Worthy*, 70.

55. Krystal Sarasin, *Your Subconscious Mind: 4-Part Online Course*, Bedford Integrative Therapeutic Services Ltd., 2024, Online course.

56. Sarasin, *Your Subconscious Mind*.

57. Shawn Johnson, *Attacking Anxiety: From Panicked and Depressed to Alive and Free* (Nashville: Thomas Nelson, 2022).

58. Johnson, *Attacking Anxiety*, 64.

59. Johnson, *Attacking Anxiety*, 212.

60. Alain Robert, "The best view comes after the hardest climb," accessed October 25, 2025, https://www.visitsoutheastengland.com/be-inspired/blog/2024/5/22/12-breathtaking-views-in-south-east-england-a2509.

61. Quotation attributed to Fred DeVito.

62. Omartian, *The Power of a Praying Woman 365-Day Desk Calendar*, March 31.

63. Radmacher, Mary Anne. 2022. *Courage Doesn't Always Roar: And Sometimes It Does—Re-Defining Courage with Daily Inspirations*. Turner Publishing.

64. Omartian, *The Power of a Praying Woman 365-Day Desk Calendar*, March 31.

65. Healthline, "How to Release 'Emotional Baggage' and the Tension That Goes with It," Aug 19, 2024, https://www.healthline.com.

66. Solex, "AO Scan Technology," https://www.solexglobal.com/ao-scan. .

67. Solex, "Inner Voice," https://www.solexglobal.com/innervoice.

68. Red Rocks Austin, "Drug of Choice // Doug Wekenman," YouTube video, 49:35, Sep 10, 2023, YouTube.com.

69. Susan Peirce Thompson, *Bright Line Eating: The Science of Living Happy, Thin, and Free* (Carlsbad, CA: Hay House, Inc., 2017).

70. Thompson, *Bright Line Eating*, 35.

71. Thompson, *Bright Line Eating*, 55.

72. Thompson, *Bright Line Eating*, 76.

73. Thompson, *Bright Line Eating*, 77.

74. Cara Whitney, *Unbridled Faith Devotions for Young Readers* (Nashville: Tommy Nelson, 2020), 102.

75. Voskamp, *WayMaker*, 113.

76. *Personality Module: Personality/Leadership Styles*, Protestant Women of the Chapel, accessed October 25, 2025.

77. Smalley Institute, "Personality Test."

78. Lee Strobel, *The Case for Faith: A Journalist Investigates the Toughest Objections to Christianity* (Grand Rapids, MI: Zondervan, 2000), 46–47.

79. *Our Daily Bread Devotional Collection* (Grand Rapids, MI: Our Daily Bread Ministries, n.d.), September 10.

80. Zach Williams with Robert Noland, *Rescue Story: Faith, Freedom, and Finding My Way Home* (Grand Rapids, MI: Zondervan, 2024), 208.

81. Williams and Noland, *Rescue Story*, 210.

82. Shawn Johnson, Red Rocks Church, sermon.

83. Omartian, *The Power of a Praying Woman 365-Day Desk Calendar*, September 14.

84. Richard G. Tedeschi and Lawrence G. Calhoun, "Posttraumatic Growth: Conceptual Foundations and Empirical Evidence," *Psychological Inquiry* 15, no. 1 (2004): 1–18.

85. Mark Batterson, *The Circle Maker: Praying Circles Around Your Biggest Dreams and Greatest Fears* (Zondervan, 2016).